DUTCH OVEN FAVORITES

MORE OF THE BEST OF THE BLACK POT

MARK HANSEN

HOBBLE CREEK PRESS
An imprint of Cedar Fort, Inc.
Springville, Utah

ISBN 13: 978-1-4621-1898-4

Published by Hobble Creek Press, an imprint of Cedar Fort, Inc.
2373 W. 700 S., Springville, UT 84663
Distributed by Cedar Fort, Inc., www.cedarfort.com

LIBRARY OF CONGRESS CONTROL NUMBER: 2016940472

Cover design by M. Shaun McMurdie
Cover design © 2016 Cedar Fort, Inc.

Printed in the United States of America

10 9 8 7 6 5 4 3 2 1

CONTENTS

MY DUTCH OVEN STORY

MY JOURNEY INTO THE WORLD OF DUTCH OVENING, and even into cooking and cookbook writing, began as a surprise.

My dear wife surprised me with a gift of a 12-inch Lodge dutch oven for Father's Day in 2006.

Before that time, I barely knew how to cook indoors, much less face the challenges of outdoor cooking. Honestly, I wasn't particularly interested in learning either.

But this was a new challenge that gave me the chance to learn something cool, and I got excited. So, I accepted the challenge and researched recipes online. I also learned how to season my dutch oven. The first thing I tried was pizza, because I remembered doing pizza in a dutch oven as a Boy Scout, but I didn't remember how it was done.

The first time I used my dutch oven, the recipe consisted of a box mix for the crust, and pizza sauce from a jar, both of which I would never do now! Nonetheless, it was a success! My kids loved it, my wife was impressed, and I was on my way.

I decided then to begin cooking all of our family's Sunday dinners out on the back porch. I'd look up recipes online, try them out, and use my family as my tasting lab. As I started to get the hang of it after a few tries, I started to get that false beginner's confidence, and I tried more complex things, like breads and pies. I quickly learned that there was much for me to learn!

But I always retained my desire to explore and cook things that were not commonly done in an outdoor dutch oven. That fed my drive for learning, and I really grew as a cook.

Soon after that, a friend suggested that I blog my recipes. I had already been running a few blogs, so I thought, *I need another blog like I need another hole in my head!* It wasn't long before I was blogging about dutch ovens at marksblackpot.com. It is now the oldest continuously running dutch oven blog on the Internet.

After a few years of what I thought was simple fun on my back porch and in the blog, my publisher invited me to consider authoring a cookbook. I don't claim to be an expert, and I'm not trained in classical culinary techniques. However, I've learned a lot from my newfound love of dutch oven cooking, and I'm excited to share what I've learned. I hope you'll join me for the ride.

HOW TO USE THIS BOOK

FAIR WARNING: The recipes in this book are all about using a cast iron, camp-style dutch oven that uses charcoal for a heat source. You can use a cast iron dutch oven in your in-home stove or oven. Just be aware that you will need to adjust the temperatures and the cook times accordingly, but that's not what this book is intended for. You could also use an aluminum dutch oven instead of a cast iron one. If you do, you'll want to adjust the number of coals and turn your dutch ovens more often to prevent hot spots. Again, this book is not designed for these alternatives.

This book is really an extension of my first cookbook, *Best of the Black Pot*, which largely consists of recipes from my blog, marksblackpot.com. It's really just a good, all-around collection of some of my favorite dutch oven dishes that I've done over the years.

A lot of basic information is found in this book that many reading it might already be aware of, especially if you've read any of my previous cookbooks or my blog. This includes things like how to buy a good dutch oven, how to season or reseason it, how to count out and use the coals, what other kinds of equipment to buy, and other basic information. This is important stuff, but many will want to jump right to the recipes. For that reason, I've added all of these things into the final chapter, simply labeled "General Dutch Oven and Cooking Info."

A note on pictures. I love to have pictures in my cookbooks. I love to see what the final dish might look like. Unfortunately, having beautiful, full-color pictures throughout the pages can exponentially increase the price of the book. So, to keep it more affordable for you, we've decided to use tech as a compromise. At the beginning of many of the recipes, you will find a funny looking box. This is called a QR code. Your smart phone or tablet might have a scanner app, and if it does, just open that the app and point the camera at the QR code box. It will scan the box and open a picture of that recipe.

To get the most from this book, browse the recipes and see what interests you. Then give some of them a try. When you do, visit marksblackpot.com and leave a comment. Tell us how they turned out!

CHAPTER 1

EASY DUTCH OVEN RECIPES

KEEP IT SIMPLE!

A LONG TIME AGO, a friend of mine and I were talking, and he asked me to give him some good, simple recipes. His church group was having a dutch oven event, and he wanted to get in on it. He wanted something that was delicious and fancy-tasting, but not difficult to pull off or overwhelming for a novice chef.

That got me thinking. I know a lot of really good, simple recipes, and I ought to put together a series of blog posts on them. It's also good for a first chapter in a recipe book. It's wise to start out with the easy ones and then move on to more complex, difficult recipes in other chapters.

I did some digging and came up with some recipes in three categories.

- One-pot, one-step meals: These are dishes that are full and hearty and simple to do. You assemble the ingredients right in the dutch oven, put it on the coals, and cook your food. Simple, clean, easy.
- Two-step meals: These are dishes that have an extra preparatory step. You might have to brown the meat before adding all the other ingredients, for example. You might have to cook something in one pot and then add more to it for the final cooking.
- Easy breads: Breads have lots of steps and are tricky to cook, so I made a separate category for them.

Even though I'm trying to keep things simple, I'm also trying to make them from scratch as much as possible. It's easy to pour ingredients from cans and heat them up, but I find it much more satisfying to go deep and make things as much on my own as possible.

I also want to dispel the idea that *simple* is *bland*. You can take easy dishes with few steps, and with some cool spices and flavors, make them elegant and special.

ONE-POT, ONE-STEP MEALS

A SIMPLE BEEF STEW WITH EVERYTHING

Tools

12-inch dutch oven
18–20 coals below

Ingredients

2 Tbsp. oil
1–2 lbs. stew beef
2 medium to large potatoes, quartered
  and sliced
1 cup sliced mushrooms
2 sweet peppers, chopped
  (I like to use one green and one of
  a different color, like red or yellow.
  It adds more color and a slightly
  different flavor.)

1–2 large carrots, sliced
1–2 celery stalks, sliced
2 medium tomatoes, chopped
1 jalapeno, seeded, cored, and
  sliced
1/2 Tbsp. crushed bay leaves (or
  crumble a few whole leaves)
1 Tbsp. parsley
1/2 Tbsp. thyme
2 Tbsp. minced garlic
liberal shakes (maybe 1/6 cup)
  balsamic vinegar
1 (14 oz.) can beef broth
salt
pepper
2 Tbsp. flour (added at the end)

This stew is in category one—a one-pot, one-step meal. Sometimes I call these dump meals, because you just dump everything into the dutch oven and cook it!

I started by lighting up about 25 coals. There will be extras to help with lighting fresh coals. While those were heating up, I prepared the dutch oven inside. I put a little oil at the bottom of the 12-inch dutch oven, along with the beef at the bottom. Then I started chopping and slicing veggies. I just added everything into the dutch oven directly, stirring it up as I went. You can make this with just about any veggies you happen to have in the fridge. I think the only ones that are "required" are the potatoes and onions, and maybe the carrots.

With all the veggies and meat in, I poured in the can of broth and added the salt and pepper. I'd keep adding salt and pepper to taste throughout the cooking process. It doesn't really matter what order you put things in. It's all going into the same pot, and then it gets added to the heat.

I took the pot outside onto the front porch and spread out about 18 to 20 coals on my cooking area (a small metal table) and set the dutch oven (with the lid on) on top of it. Within 15 to 20 minutes, it was boiling, so I removed a few coals (maybe 4 or so) to reduce the heat a little. I still had some coals going in my side fire, and I added some to it from the bag from time to time to be able to have hot ones to replenish the ones under the dutch oven.

Every half hour or so I'd open the lid and stir the stew. Having that much liquid, and cooking mainly from the bottom, makes this dish an easy one to learn on, since regulating the heat isn't that tricky. As the coals died down, I'd add new ones from my side fire. The total cooking time was an hour and a half to two hours. My gauge is the potatoes. When they're done, I'm safe, though I usually cook it a bit longer for more flavors.

Just at the end, I added the flour as a thickener. I imagine I could have added it at the beginning and it probably would have been okay, but I think it maintains the thickness better when added at the end. I've heard that tapioca powder is a really good thickener, which can be added at the beginning.

This is a yummy basic stew. To take this to another level, put the dutch oven on the coals with just the oil. Let it heat up a bit, and then brown the meat, onions, garlic, and mushrooms. Once they are browned, add everything else. Also, when you serve it, garnish it with a few crumbs of feta cheese!

CHICKEN AND POTATOES

I remember the night when my son Brendon and I did a demo for our church's women's group. They invited me to demonstrate dutch oven cooking, so, I did my old standby of chicken, onions, and potatoes.

Brendon and I did a short twenty-minute demo where we poured all the ingredients into the dutch oven. While the ladies attended other classes, we put it on the coals to cook. After the evening was done, they all came back and sampled.

This is one of the most flexible meals you could ever cook. The ingredients can adjust to whatever you have on hand, including the spices and flavorings. You can prepare it in stages or as a dump meal, where you just dump everything into the dutch oven and cook it. It's kind of like a good jazz tune. It comes out different every time I cook it.

That night, we went herbal, and we made it simple.

This recipe serves about 4–6 people, and can be done in a standard 12-inch dutch oven.

BASIC MEATS AND VEGGIES

Tools

8–10 coals below
16–18 coals above

Ingredients

a few Tbsp. of olive oil
2–3 medium to large onions, sliced
3–4 boneless chicken breasts, cubed
3–4 potatoes, quartered and sliced
2–3 carrots, sliced
3–4 stalks of celery, sliced

2–3 sweet peppers, sliced
about a half pound of bacon,
    cooked crispy
flavorings (herbal-style)
    1 heaping Tbsp. minced garlic
    liberal shakes of
    parsley
    rosemary
    oregano
a few shakes (about a tsp. or so)
    balsamic vinegar
and, of course, salt and pepper

We started by lighting 25–30 coals before the demo. While those were getting glowing and hot, we sliced up our ingredients. Since we chose a simple dish, we put everything into the dutch oven and put on the lid. We made a ring of about 8–10 coals and set the oven on top. Then we put about 16–18 coals in a ring around the top of the lid.

I left a few coals burning aside. After about 10–15 minutes, I put about ten fresh coals on those. They got lit, and by the time the coals on the dutch oven had burned down, they were ready to be replenished.

We cooked it for about 45 minutes, stirring every 15 minutes, until the chicken and the veggies were done. We checked the softness of the potatoes as a good gauge of doneness.

Here are a couple other suggestions for flavoring combinations.

SOME LIKE IT HOT

Ingredients

1 heaping Tbsp. minced garlic

1–2 jalapeno peppers, sliced. If you don't like it really hot, you can seed and core them first, or use fewer peppers

a few shakes of cayenne pepper, chili powder, or Louisiana-style hot sauce (Tabasco)

a few shakes of paprika

about 1/2 bunch of fresh chopped cilantro

juice of 1–2 limes

salt and pepper

or, just pour in your favorite salsa instead of or in addition to the above ingredients

SPRINGTIME LEMON

Ingredients

1 heaping Tbsp. minced garlic

1/2 cup fresh chopped parsley

zest of 1 lemon

juice of 1–2 lemons

salt and pepper

Here's how to kick it up a notch and make it even more delicious!

Cook the bacon in the dutch oven over 15–20 coals. (Make sure it's good and crispy.) Then remove most of the grease. Sauté the onions and garlic in the bacon grease until they're translucent and sweet. Add the remaining ingredients and cook as above.

Another great idea is that after you take the dutch oven off the coals, just a few minutes before serving, coat the food with a layer of your favorite shredded cheese. Let the oven's residual heat melt it. For the herbal flavorings, I'd recommend mozzarella. For the hot and spicy version, cheddar or colby jack. With the lemon style, I'd crumble feta onto the dish once it's served.

BBQ CHICKEN

Another simple and traditional dutch oven favorite is barbecue chicken. At its easiest, you simply thaw some frozen chicken breasts, put them in the oven, smother them in your favorite commercial barbecue sauce, and bake them until they're done.

It can be served as is, or pulled apart with forks and served on buns for a delicious sandwich.

Here's a version that picks the flavors up a bit but is still simple.

Tools

12-inch shallow dutch oven
10–12 coals below
18–22 coals above

Ingredients

chicken for 3–5 people (3–5 chicken
    breasts, 3–5 entire chicken legs, or
    6–10 chicken thighs), thawed.
1 medium yellow onion
1 green bell pepper
2 (14 oz.) cans of beans (different kinds)
1 (18 oz.) bottle barbecue sauce
    (or see the recipe to the right)

Barbecue Sauce

Ingredients

1 (8 oz.) can tomato sauce
1 (6 oz.) can tomato paste
3–5 Tbsp. mustard
3–5 Tbsp. molasses
liberal shakes of
    salt
    black pepper
    garlic powder
    paprika
    and a touch of chili powder

I start this dish off by thawing the chicken, patting the chicken dry, and firing up the coals. I lightly season the chicken on both sides with a bit of salt and pepper. While that's being absorbed and the coals are heating up, I'll dice the onion and the pepper. If I'm using a homemade sauce (see recipe above and instructions below), I would mix that now too.

I drain the beans and add them, along with the onions and the peppers into the dutch oven, stirring it all up. I layer the chicken over the bean mixture and cover the chicken using the entire bottle of barbecue sauce. (If you're using the homemade sauce, see the recipe above and the instructions below.)

Then, I put the lid on and set it on the 10–12 coals, which should be in a circle around the bottom of the dutch oven. Add a ring of 18–22 coals on the outer edge of the lid. I cook it until the internal temperature of the chicken is about 170, which is probably about 45 minutes to an hour. The barbecue sauce will bake onto the chicken and drizzle down into the beans, making a delicious, full meal.

If you want to make a delicious barbecue sauce, here's my process. All BBQ sauces are made of four basic ingredients: tomatoes, a sweetener, an acid, and seasonings. Armed with this understanding, you can be inventive with your own sauce. A common sweetener is brown sugar, but I've seen people use fruit marmalades. Vinegar works for the acid. Some will use a cola for both the sweetener and the acid.

In my house recipe, I use mustard and molasses. I also use my own taste rather than measuring. I start by emptying the tomato paste and tomato sauce into a bowl, mixing it up thoroughly, and tasting it to get a baseline flavor on my palate. Then, I stir in mustard, one or two tablespoons at a time, until the tang is equal to the tomato, and neither overpowers the other. After that, I'll do the same with the molasses. Once these three are harmoniously balanced, then I know I've got a good basic sauce, and it's just a matter of adding in flavorings to enhance it. I add salt, pepper, garlic powder, etc., based on my whimsy and what I have available, stirring and tasting all along the way. When it's set to your liking, cover and chill it for a while so the flavors will blend. Then use it as you would the commercial sauce.

A homemade sauce on basic chicken is a great way to personalize a tasty and easy dinner.

CHILI

"THROW IT ALL IN THE DUTCH OVEN" CHILI

A few years ago, our church congregation had a chili cook-off. It brought out the chef in everyone, it seemed, and I got a lot of ideas as I tasted everyone's chili. One thing I learned is that you really can't go wrong. There are so many different chilies, with so many different flavorings and ingredients, that there really isn't a wrong way to do it. Here are a few tricks, along with my own take on this classic, one-pot meal.

One trick is to add cinnamon. This yummy spice adds a different kick that you don't expect but are sure to enjoy. Other flavorings I like include lemon juice and cilantro, as well as molasses.

Another cool trick is, toward the end of the cooking, to add about a half cup of corn masa or crushed corn chips. It thickens up the broth with a rich flavor and aroma.

Other than that, it's pretty much the same as any other chili. There are a few key ingredients, and the rest of it is simply whatever you have on hand. Chili is one of those things that you can make with a pretty wide variety of ingredients. And the experimenting never stops.

Tools

12-inch dutch oven
20+ coals underneath

Essential Ingredients

1 lb. ground beef or other meat
2–3 medium onions
3 (15 oz.) cans beans with liquid
(different kinds of beans)
2 (14.5 oz.) cans tomatoes with liquid

1/2 cup corn masa harina or crushed tortilla chips

Other things I sometimes like to add (but you can add whatever you'd like)

2 Tbsp. garlic
1–2 jalapeno peppers, cored and seeded, chopped
2–3 bell peppers

(Other things to add cont. on following page.)

(Other things to add cont. from previous page)

liberal amounts of
  parsley
  cilantro
  salt
  pepper
  cumin
  cinnamon

More things you can add

celery
crushed red peppers
lemon juice
brown sugar
barbecue sauce
molasses

To prepare chili, I only use bottom heat. I'll light up the coals, and once they get a bit white, I'll arrange them with a bit of space between under the dutch oven. I start by browning the meat. I might also sauté the onions and peppers, but that's not absolutely necessary.

Then, when the meat is done, I'll add in the onions, the beans, and the tomatoes. Sometimes, I'll drain one or two cans of the beans. Occasionally I'll put the lid on, because that will bring the chili to a simmer more quickly. Once it's simmering, you can start adding in other ingredients, stirring and tasting as you go.

It will be ready in as little as 30–45 minutes, but the longer it simmers, the more the flavors will blend.

DUTCH OVEN DUMP CAKE COBBLER

For a picture of this recipe, scan this QR code:

Dump cake cobblers, for the uninitiated, is a dutch oven tradition. You put some canned peaches with their juice in the bottom of the dutch oven, and then you shake a cake mix on top. Sometimes, you put butter on top of the floating mix. As it cooks, the juices boil up and mix with the cake mix, and the butter (if you added any) melts down into the bubbling mire. Cool (just a little) and serve with ice cream.

Let me make a confession. I've never really liked to cook dump cake cobblers.

I'm of this opinion for two reasons: 1) Everybody does them. And everyone I talk to about dutch oven cooking remembers having one once and it tasted "so good." No matter how much I talk about fancy meats and elaborate desserts, someone always says, "Yeah, but can you do a cobbler like that?"

And that leads me to number 2) For a while, I couldn't do them! For some reason, they never turned out the way I wanted them to. They were either too runny and sloppy, or the cake mix never mixed, and I ended up with dried out powder on top.

I figured that there were two issues that were preventing me from getting the perfect dump cake cobbler each time. One was the balance of peach syrup to how much cake mix was on top, and the other was the placement of the heat to make it boil up properly.

Part of the problem in the past was that since *everybody* does these desserts, *everybody* does them just a little differently. So, resolving the issue by research didn't get me anywhere. I had to experiment. Finally, I found the balance of all the factors. The crust on top was an actual crusty cake, not a dry powder. The peaches on the bottom were nicely blended in with the cake. It tasted great!

So, here's the result.

Tools

12-inch shallow dutch oven
12 coals below
12 coals above

Ingredients

2 (15 oz.) cans peaches in light syrup
2 boxes yellow cake mix
1/4 cup brown sugar
liberal shakes of cinnamon
and nutmeg
1 stick butter

I start (after lighting up some coals) by opening the cans of peaches and pouring them, with the syrup, directly into the dutch oven. Then, I open up the boxes and bags of cake mix and sprinkle them over the peaches and syrup.

After many tries, I've decided that there should be a 1:1 ratio between cans of syrup and boxes of cake mix. I also discovered that one box of cake mix is not enough in a 12-inch dutch oven. If I were doing this in a 10-inch dutch oven, I would half everything.

Next I crumble the brown sugar over the top of the cake mix and sprinkle on the spices. The final ingredient is to cut the stick of butter into small pieces and scatter these over the crust as well. Then, the lid goes on, and the whole dutch oven goes on the coals.

Now, if I were baking a normal dessert, I would put more coals on top, and fewer coals on the bottom. In this case, however, I want more heat on the bottom to get the peach juice boiling up to blend with the cake mix.

I bake it for about 35 minutes before checking it, rotating it once along the way. When you rotate a dutch oven, lift it by the bail and turn it a quarter turn in either direction. Then set it back down, doing the same for the lid. This repositions the food in relation to the coals and prevents burning. Determining the doneness is tricky. It should be brown on top, and the liquid should have boiled up through the crust. I figure it would be hard to burn it, so I sometimes let it go as much as 10 minutes longer.

Then, I bring it in and let it cool. This not only keeps it from burning my guests' mouths, but it also gives the boiling syrup and the cake mix more time to settle together. Finally, we top it with ice cream and eat it. Following this pattern, it comes out exactly as I had always wanted it to be. A nice crust on top, a little bit runny blend underneath, and delicious peaches as a base. The sugar and the butter add a little crispiness and flavor, and the spices take it to a new level.

The added taste of victory is especially sweet!

DUTCH OVEN DROP BISCUITS

I actually like drop biscuits a lot, because you don't have to handle them much. You mix them, you scoop them out with a spoon, and you drop them into the hot dutch oven. No folding, no rolling—just simple, bready goodness.

Tools

12-inch dutch oven
10 coals below
22 coals above

Ingredients

2 cups flour
1/2 cup (1 stick) cold, unsalted
      butter, cut into small pieces
1 Tbsp. baking powder
1 tsp. salt
1 cup whole milk

I start by lighting up the coals and lightly oiling the inside of my oven. When the coals are getting white edges, I put them in the ring and set the oven on top. I set the remaining coals on the lid and leave it to preheat.

Mixing the ingredients is easy. I start with the flour, and I cut in the butter. The easiest way is with a pastry knife, but I've seen people do it just by crisscrossing two butter knives like they're sword fighting themselves.

You can use your hands to blend the flour and the butter, but don't overwork it. You'll be raising the temperature of the butter, and it's best if the dough stays cool so that the butter fats can trap more of the gas and get more lift. If you do use your hands, chill the dough for a while after mixing.

I continue to chop and mix while I add the rest of the dry ingredients. Finally, the dough will look like coarse meal. I pour in the milk and stir it all up with my trusty wooden spoon. Actually, since we're not dealing with yeast germs, you could use just about any kind of spoon. But I still prefer my wooden utensils.

I remove the lid. I scoop out a spoonful of dough and drop it into the bottom of the oven. It might sizzle a bit. I keep dropping dough until I either run out of room or dough. Then, I put on the lid, add the coals to the top, and bake it. I'll check the biscuits in about 15 minutes. Usually, they are done by then or very close to it, but sometimes, they need a few more minutes.

When they're nice and golden, take the oven off the coals, scoop the biscuits out with a plastic spatula, and serve them. They can be served right away, or you can wait until other dishes are done and serve them cool.

CHAPTER 2

CHICKEN, TURKEY, AND POULTRY

I LOVE COOKING POULTRY for so many reasons. One is, of course, the health benefits. Chicken is a lean meat, so there's a lot less fat. It's also less expensive than beef.

What I like most about chicken is that the flavor is rich but relatively neutral. As a result, you can do so much with it. You can match up many different flavors and vegetables with it, and it will still be delicious. You can have it be the main focus of a meal, or it can be an ingredient in a soup or mash.

I hope that after trying a few of these recipes, you'll be convinced as well!

SIMPLE DUTCH OVEN ROAST CHICKEN

Roasting a chicken in a dutch oven is an easy thing to do. It looks complex, but it's not. The end result is delicious and can easily feed a family, probably even with a little left over.

The last time I did this, it reminded me of how wonderful and impressive it is.

Tools

12-inch deep dutch oven
10–12 coals below
14–16 coals above

Ingredients

1 whole chicken (thawed, if you
    bought it frozen)
salt
pepper
paprika
dried parsley
dried rosemary
dried sage
a touch of crushed red pepper
oil

2–3 large potatoes
2–3 medium to large onions.

1 (14 oz.) can green beans (optional)
1 (14 oz.) can whole corn (optional)

First, I got the coals lit and let them get white and hot. Then, I got the chicken ready. I opened the package and let the chicken drain. I patted it dry with paper towels. I poked the skin over the breast and the legs with holes so the juices and flavors could penetrate to the meat under the skin.

I sprinkled on the seasonings and drizzled on a little oil. I rubbed the oil over the surface of the chicken. I don't list amounts here, because I didn't really pay attention to how much I put in as I was sprinkling them over the bird. Just be liberal, except with the red pepper. Be more cautious with the pepper, if you don't like it hot.

If you're the more precise type of chef, you could mix the spices as a blend first, tasting along the way, to get the exact blend you want.

Then, while the chicken was resting to absorb the seasonings, I cubed up the potatoes and the onions into 1- or 3/4-inch blocks and tossed them into the bottom of the dutch oven. This flavors the dish and lifts the chicken up above the heat and the juices as it cooks. Plus, the potatoes and onions make great sides.

I put the dutch oven onto the coals and started cooking. This is a fun kind of cooking, because I sit there and watch the coals burn. It's not a bad idea to stay with it, because you're going to need to replenish the coals from time to time.

I cooked it for about two hours total, to an internal temperature of 175 to 180 degrees. In a traditional indoor oven, cooking it that long will usually dry it out. But in a dutch oven, the juices are all trapped under the heavy lid. Not only is the meat done and tender, but it also falls off the bones, and the connecting tissue is broken down.

If you want some veggies as a side dish, the easiest way to do that is to drain a can of green beans and a can of corn, mix them together, and pour them around the sides of the chicken when there's only about 15–20 minutes left in the cooking.

An even better option would be to use fresh beans and fresh corn. If you do that, snap the beans and shuck the corn. You could either cut the corn off the cob, or break the cobs into short lengths. If you use fresh veggies, add them when there are 30–45 minutes left in the cook time.

DUTCH OVEN ARTICHOKE AND VEGGIE CHICKEN

For a picture of this recipe, scan this QR code:

My wife and I were recently invited to attend an awards dinner. Unfortunately, we weren't the ones receiving an award! Someday, I'll get to thank the Academy and all the little people that have helped me along the way . . .!

But the dinner was great! It was this delicious chicken breast surrounded by veggies. It had a bit of citrus and acidic twang to it. So, I thought I'd give it a try in my dutch ovens, along with some variations. These mostly come in the form of the various veggies you can add in, depending on what you've got.

I decided to serve it all on a bed of brown rice, which was also different from the formal dinner we attended.

Tools

12-inch dutch oven
24+ coals below for searing stage
10–12 below for baking stage
24–26 above

8-inch dutch oven
12+ coals below

Ingredients

6–8 boneless, skinless chicken breasts
  (We buy them frozen in a bag.
  Make sure they are well thawed.)
olive oil
salt
pepper
paprika
garlic powder
dried parsley
dried oregano
2–3 medium to large potatoes
1–2 medium to large onions

vegetables to put on top
  1 bottle or can (about 14 oz.)
    brined or pickled artichoke hearts
  15–20 cherry tomatoes
  2–3 stalks celery
  2–3 carrots

1–2 lemons

2 cups brown rice
4 cups water
a cube of chicken bullion
salt

I prepared the chicken while the coals and the dutch oven were getting hot. I made sure that the chicken was well thawed and patted it dry with paper towels. One problem with chicken breasts is that the middle is much thicker than the edges, so it's a little more difficult to regulate the cooking. So, I would pound the chicken a little thinner with one of those meat tenderizer mallets. Not so flat like you do for a cordon bleu or some other kind of roll-up, but just so it's not so thick in the middle. Then I drizzled on some oil and rubbed in the spices and herbs on both sides.

I put a lot (a couple dozen) of coals underneath my dutch oven, and I let it get really hot, with a little oil drizzled on the bottom.

Once it was hot, I set in 3–4 of the breasts and let them sear a little on each side. Then, I pulled them out, let the dutch oven heat up again (you might even want to replenish the coals), and I finished the remaining 3–4 breasts. They should have a little brown on them, and the spice rub should be nicely cooked on. It's okay if it's not cooked all the way through though. We're going to bake it.

Then, I set up the dutch oven with the coals configured for baking (the second set of numbers above). I cubed the potatoes into large chunks, about 3/4 to 1 inch big. Then I cut up the onions into big 1/8-inch chunks. By that, I mean, I cut each onion in half, and then each half into quarters. All of these got tossed into the bottom of the dutch oven and stirred up a bit to coat them with the oil.

On top of that, I layered the browned chicken breasts, and I arranged them so that they were overlapping as little as possible. I put on the lid and added the coals on top for baking, using the coal count under "Tools" on the opposite page.

Then I sliced up the other veggies. They should be sliced thin on the bias so there isn't much thickness and they can cook more quickly. I chopped and diced the artichoke hearts coarsely, just to make the bits a little smaller. I cut the cherry tomatoes in half once. Then, I opened the dutch oven and scattered all of these over the chicken breasts. I poured the artichoke brine over the chicken as well, and, after zesting one of the lemons, added the zest and the juice of the lemons as well. I let that cook for about a half hour.

Making the rice is easy too. I added the rice, the bouillon, salt, and the water to the 8-inch dutch oven and set it, with the lid on, on the coals specified. I watched for it to start venting steam out from the side of the lid, showing me that it was boiling. I gave it another 10–12 minutes before removing it from the coals. Without lifting the lid, I set it aside to cool down and finish cooking. I let it go for a while, because brown rice takes longer to cook than white rice. I had to resist the temptation to lift the lid and check it! I wanted the steam to stay in there and cook the rice.

When it was all done and ready to serve, it smelled delicious and looked great. I spread some rice on the plate and added the chicken breast and the veggies. I scooped a bit of potato and onion onto the plate and drizzled some of the broth liquid from the bottom of the dutch oven over the entire entrée. It was a great meal!

THANKSGIVING TURKEY IN A DUTCH OVEN

For a picture of this recipe, scan this QR code:

You know, there are so many ways to do a turkey, and so many recipes, that it's just amazing! I've been reading through the Internet forums with all the ideas, methods, and recipes, and it's just mind-boggling. While I'm giving thanks, I'll give all my friends out there some good thanks for all their advice and help this last year.

This particular year, I did the same herbal roast turkey that I did for Christmas in previous years. Then, in the 12-inch deep dutch oven, I did a ham recipe of my own design. I'll write the recipes up separate, even though I roasted them concurrently. The Dutch Oven Ham recipe is found on page 59.

Tools

14-inch deep dutch oven
15–18 coals on top
24–28 coals below

Turkey
Ingredients

13 lb. turkey
2 more tsp. minced garlic
salt
1 cup water

Turkey Stuffing
Ingredients

1 onion, quartered
3–4 slices bread (I used sourdough rye)
3 Tbsp. melted butter
12 bay leaf
2 tsp. minced garlic
salt
pepper (I like it coarse ground)

I started out with the turkey and began by mixing the stuffing ingredients and removing the neck and giblets and the various pouches that the company sticks in the turkey. I'd kept it in the fridge to thaw for the last few days and took it out early in the morning. I wanted to have it on the coals by 10:00 in order to get it on the table by 2:30 or 3:00, including carving time. A 13-pound turkey isn't going to have very much room for stuffing, so I didn't really do that much. I set the turkey in the 14-inch dutch oven. Then I rubbed the additional minced garlic onto the body and sprinkled some salt over it. I added a cup of water to the dutch oven for steaming, and closed it up. I put it on the coals.

Basting Sauce
Ingredients

1/2 cup butter
1 tsp. dried mint leaves
1/2 tsp. dried thyme
1/2 tsp. dried sage
1/2 tsp. dried marjoram
1/2 tsp. sweet basil
1 tsp. celery salt
1 tsp. salt

In the 8-inch dutch oven, I combined all of the basting sauce ingredients, and simply set that on top of the turkey dutch oven lid, using those upper coals to melt the butter and simmer the sauce.

From then on, it was simply a matter of keeping the coals fresh and basting the turkey occasionally. The total cooking time was about four hours.

Veggies
Ingredients

7 medium potatoes, sliced
2–3 carrots, peeled and sliced

About an hour to an hour and a half from serving time, I sliced up the potatoes and the carrots and just dumped them in around the bird.

I didn't bother with mashing the potatoes, I just served them alongside. Someone else in the family brought the mashed potatoes, anyway.

Some folks I'd been talking to mentioned that a dutch oven turkey doesn't brown up like an oven-baked turkey. While that's true, I found that this one did brown up nicely on top. I imagine that's because of it's proximity to the lid with coals on. I did try and keep the coals toward the edges rather than in the middle of the lid so it wouldn't burn.

BACON-DRAPED TURKEY

For a picture of this recipe, scan this QR code:

Christmas dinner is always a fun time for me. Some may look at all the cooking as a lot of extra fuss, and it is, but it's fuss that I enjoy. I'll often do a turkey, and sometimes a ham, depending on how many are coming over. I really like the smaller turkeys. Not only do they fit in the dutch oven better, but they're more tender and juicy. I have two 14-inch-deep dutch ovens, and I can get a 12–13 pound turkey hen easily into one of them and have room for veggies on the side. I did this one a new way, draped in bacon. It was delicious. Here's the process.

Tools

14-inch dutch oven
14–16 coals below
20–22 coals above

8-inch dutch oven
10 coals below

Ingredients

1 12–14 lb. turkey hen
13 oz. salt (about half of a 26 oz. carton)

1 (1 lb.) pkg. brown sugar
water to cover

2–3 large potatoes
2–3 medium onions
salt
pepper
cayenne pepper
1 lb. sliced bacon

some of the turkey broth
2 Tbsp. flour
1/2 cup water

A few days before the big day, I started thawing the turkey. The best way to do that is to move it from the freezer to the fridge. We were having 30–40 degree days, so I just set it in the garage, still in its plastic packaging.

The night before cooking, I set up the brine. This is going to be an overnight soak in a salt water solution to tenderize the meat and give it a bit of tang. I usually do this in a travel cooler. The best I've found is the large, round drink coolers, but you can use whatever you've got. I started by putting in about two inches of hot tap water in the bottom. To that, I added the salt and the sugar. I stirred this all up and got it as dissolved as I could. Then, I added a few more inches of cold water, stirring as I went.

I unpacked the turkey and stuck a lot of holes in the skin all around with a paring knife. This helps the brine get more into the meat. I set it in the water (which actually looks really gross with the brown sugar in it), and then poured in enough water to cover the turkey. As a last bit, I usually add in some ice before closing up the lid. I always do that in the summer so that it stays cool overnight. In the winter, I just let the cold of the night in the garage keep it the right temperature.

By morning it was nicely brined and evenly thawed, ready for the fire.

Since this was to be served in the early evening, I started preparing it at about eleven o'clock. I first cubed up the potatoes into one-inch blocks and tossed them around the bottom of the lightly oiled dutch oven. I repeated this with the onions. You could add more veggies if you wanted, like celery and carrots. The point of the potatoes is to lift the turkey up above the juices that cook out. Then I went out and lit up a chimney full of coals.

I set the turkey onto the potatoes and onions. Then I sprinkled some salt, pepper, and paprika over the upper surface of the bird.

Finally, I simply draped the bacon strips over the top of the turkey. There were sufficient strips to layer them twice—once across the chest, and once lengthwise. When that was done, it was time to start roasting!

I went out and set it on the coals. Typically, when roasting, you do the same number below and above, but I usually go a few more above, just because heat rises, especially when it's winter and there's a breeze to blow away some of the heat. I wasn't shooting for too hot of a roasting temp, about 350 degrees. Lower than that isn't a big problem since it will just make for a slower roast, which tastes better anyway. I like to cook my turkey at an internal temperature of between 170 and 180 degrees, just to make sure it's done all the way through.

As the end approached, I got out my basting syringe and sucked up a lot of the juices from the bottom of the dutch oven. I put it into my 8-inch dutch oven and added more coals. I put the lid on but kept only bottom heat. My intent was to get it simmering.

With the lid on, it didn't take long to simmer. I mixed about two tablespoons of flour with a bit of water, enough to blend them together, but to keep it very runny. I poured some of the flour mixture into the simmering broth, and whisked for a few minutes. I watched the thickness carefully. Sometimes I've added too much flour, and it has cooked into a gel. I kept adding and stirring, waiting several minutes in between each pour, to watch for results. Before long, it was the right consistency—thick, but still fluid and not clumpy. I didn't add any seasonings since I felt that the turkey broth itself already carried much of that.

When my guests had arrived and the turkey was done, I brought it in and let it settle for a few minutes. I pulled the bacon off first, carved the meat onto a serving plate, and crumbled the bacon bits onto the turkey pieces.

The seasonings and the bacon combined for a nice flavor, which supplemented the turkey without overpowering it. It was a great centerpiece for the Christmas meal!

SORT-OF SALVADOREAN TURKEY

For a picture of this recipe, scan this QR code:

I was looking for a different, unique way to do a turkey one Thanksgiving. I'd done a lot of variations in the past, and some of them I'd done over and over. I just wanted to try something new.

I had a really good friend across the street who introduced me to his family tradition, the Salvadorean Turkey. I was intrigued, so I also looked on the web. It turns out that there are a lot of different ways of doing it, but they all have some consistent similarities. They all involve mustard sauce and tomato sauce. Many of them are like a braise in the overall mixed sauce. Others make the mustard in a baste and have the tomato in a braise. A version I was attracted to had the mustard sauce basted and browned on the skin and the tomatoes and fresh chopped veggies around the bird. After the turkey is done, the veggies are pureed and served in lieu of gravy.

That was the version I did!

A note on authenticity: Whenever there's a dish that's this traditional with this many variations, you're sure to upset someone when you do it. I don't know that what I ended up doing is a real Salvadorean turkey, and maybe someone's Salvadorean grandmother might be upset by it. Oh, well. It tasted great, and I thank the Salvadoreans for their recipes, or at least their inspiration!

Another note: Apparently, a large part of the tradition is making sandwiches using the leftover turkey and sauce in the days that follow the celebration. Sounds like a great plan to me!

Tools

14-inch deep dutch oven
16 coals below
16 coals above

Baste
Ingredients

1/2 cup mustard
1/4 cup worcestershire sauce
1/4 cup honey
a thickener, like guar gum, or just flour

Veggies
Ingredients

3–4 large potatoes
6–8 roma tomatoes
1–2 green peppers
2–3 stalks of celery
1–2 medium onions
4–5 cloves garlic, sliced
1 cup coarsely chopped green olives

Ingredients

1 (12–14 lb.) turkey hen, thawed
brine
1 lb. brown sugar
1 lb. table salt
water

Sauce
Ingredients

roasted pumpkin seeds or
    unflavored sunflower seeds in
    the husk
liberal shakes of parsley, basil,
    and oregano
a little chili powder
salt and pepper

The dish began the day before the cooking. The turkey had already been thawing for a day or two in the refrigerator. That allowed it to thaw some, but a lot of ice was still inside.

I prepared a brine bath by cleaning out a large drink cooler. A flat food cooler that you take camping will also work, as long as it's watertight. I put about a half gallon of hot water in the bottom and mixed in the salt and sugar. That's a lot of each one, I know. When that was mostly dissolved, I added enough cool water to bring it up to about halfway full. I opened up the turkey package and let it drain a bit. Then I used a fork or knife to poke some holes in the skin all around. I put the whole bird into the brine bath. I added more water until the turkey was covered. I closed up the lid nice and tight.

Now, I'm usually doing this at Thanksgiving or Christmas, so it's going to be really cool out in the garage. The bird is also usually still thawing, so it's going to keep the water really cool too. So, between the cool and salt, I don't worry too much about germs. Sometimes, however, just to be sure, I'll add some ice on top. It won't really impact the thawing, but it will help keep it cold enough to retard the germ growth and keep it out of the danger zone (above 40 degrees Fahrenheit).

The next day, cooking day, Thanksgiving Day, I got my 14-inch oven ready. I don't use it as often, so I gave it a good wiping and coated it with a quick spray of oil. I lit up some coals and let them start to get white. I pulled the turkey out of the drink cooler, drained off the brine, and put it into the dutch oven, breast up. I got out some paper towels and patted the skin surface dry. There's still a lot of moisture in the meat, and that will end up in the braising sauces.

Once the coals were getting hot, I put the dutch oven onto the coals, as written above, letting it start to roast. I also inserted a meat thermometer. Also, make sure that you have extra coals burning in a stack or in your chimney so you can start fresh ones. This will be a long, slow cook.

I mixed up the baste ingredients. It's pretty simple, and you can adjust it to your taste. I wanted it to be a thick glaze, almost a paste. Once it was mixed, I opened up the dutch oven and slathered it over all of the top and side surfaces of the turkey. I only used about a third of the mix at the time. The rest I reserved for future bastes. Then, I let it cook for about an hour. I kept refreshing the coals to keep it at a steady medium to medium-low heat.

After about an hour and a half (almost halfway through the total cook time), I started preparing the veggies, dicing and chopping as needed. The potatoes I skinned and cubed. These went in first, around the base of the turkey. The other vegetables got scattered around the sides. More baste went on top of the turkey.

During the last half of the cooking, I rebasted the turkey about every half hour to 45 minutes. It started to form a really great crust. In the last half hour or so, I put my 8-inch dutch oven on about 10–12 coals and tossed in the pumpkin or sunflower seeds with a little olive oil). I put the lid on and let them roast for 15–20 minutes, stirring occasionally. I like to get them quite brown, even a bit black, to get some smoky flavor!

When the turkey was done (at least 170 degrees, preferably 180), I brought the dutch oven in from the coals, and using meat forks, lifted it out onto a plate. I tented it with aluminum foil to preserve the heat and let it rest before carving and serving it.

The next part is a bit tricky. I scooped out the veggies and potatoes with a slotted spoon, letting them drain as I lifted them out. I separated the potatoes from the veggies as best I could. The potatoes I put into a colander to drain.

The veggies went into a blender with the herbs and other seasonings. I tossed in some of the roasted seeds—just a few to start—and gave it a spin. As I was pureeing the veggies into a sauce, I adjusted the thickness by adding more roasted seeds. You can thin it out again by adding more turkey juice from the bottom of the dutch oven.

The potatoes then went into a bowl for mashing. I added some salt and pepper to pick it up a bit. Again, if they're too dry, you can add some of the turkey juice to make them a bit more fluid.

Finally, I carved the turkey and served it up! The idea is that the diner will have a slice of turkey with some potatoes on the side and the tomato and veggie sauce drizzled over it. It's a delicious and flavorful combination, and since the bird, the potatoes, and the veggies were all cooked together, there is a nice consistent sharing of flavors between all three!

TANDOORI CHICKEN

For a picture of this recipe, scan this QR code:

    This is another one of those times when you know you're not going to get a dish exactly authentically right, but you know it will still be good. I saw this recipe online for doing tandoori chicken in a regular oven. I knew it wouldn't really work the same. A tandoor is a specialized kind of oven, with high, dry heat. You marinate your whole chicken in spices and then skewer it and stick it down the throat of this round, tapered clay oven. A home oven just won't do it authentically, and a dutch oven even more so.

    I realized that it might not be authentic tandoori chicken, but the spices would still glaze on the chicken, and it would taste great.

    Once I'd lost the worry about authenticity, it was an easy mental jump to make it in the dutch oven. There was one problem, however: the dry heat. In order for the marinade to glaze on the chicken, I would need very high and dry heat. I've done that a lot of times with the "lifted lid" or "dry roasting" technique (which I'll explain below). So, we're good to go!

    I used two whole chickens for this recipe, but the marinade could be halved to make just one.

Tools

Phase one: roasting
12-inch deep dutch oven
12–14 coals below
14–16 coals above

Phase two: dry roasting
12-inch deep dutch oven
12–14 coals below
24–28 coals above

8-inch dutch oven
10–12 coals below

Ingredients

2 medium roasting chickens, whole,
    no neck or giblets

1 cup plain yogurt
1 (6 oz.) can tomato paste
juice and zest of 1 lemon
1 tsp. hot chilli powder
1 tsp. turmeric
1 tsp. ground coriander
1 tsp. ground cumin
2 tsp. garam masala
1 tsp. ground cinnamon
2 tsp. ground ginger
2 tsp. garlic powder
salt
pepper

2–3 medium yellow onions
2–3 lemons
1 (13.5 oz.) can coconut milk
1 Tbsp. cornstarch or flour

The first task is the marinade, and I did that the night before. I mixed the yogurt and all of the spices and flavorings in a bowl. Then, I removed the chickens from their bags, drained them, and patted them dry. I also pulled out the neck and giblets. I got out a sharp slicing knife and made some slash cuts across the breast and the thighs and legs. This is so that the marinade can get down under the skin and into the meat.

I saved the big plastic bag containing the two chickens and put them back into it, pouring all of the yogurt and spices on top. I worked the bag so that the marinade covered all of the surfaces of the chicken. You could just put it in a bowl and rub it all over, finally covering it with plastic wrap. Coating the marinade on the chicken can be a messy task. This is why I like to use the bag method.

I put the coated chicken back in the fridge overnight.

When the time came to start cooking, I lit up some coals and got out my 12-inch deep oven. It might seem at first that the two chickens won't fit, but I got it to work just fine.

I quartered each onion and tossed the wedges into the bottom of the oven. I did the same to the lemons and stirred them around. These not only added flavor to the eventual gravy, but they also lifted the chicken up above the juices.

I set the marinated chickens onto the onions and lemons. I added an additional cut lemon and onion into the cavity of each chicken. Then I tucked the chickens in snugly next to each other and took the oven out to the coals.

Phase one of the cooking is just basic roasting. I let it roast for about an hour, or until the chickens came up to about 160 degrees Fahrenheit internal temperature. You might need to replenish the coals to maintain the heat during this process.

Then, in phase two of the cooking, I did the dry roasting. I opened up the lid and first extracted the juices on the bottom with a poultry baster. I added the juices to my 8-inch oven.

I prepared the 12-inch oven (with the chickens) for dry roasting. This is basically having something that raises the lid slightly so that the moisture can escape. I have a circular grill grid that's just a little larger than 12 inches, and it fits nicely over my dutch ovens. You can use other things, like nails bent into the shape of a U and hooked over the rim of the oven. Whatever raises the lid a little.

Since the moisture is no longer trapped, the heat isn't trapped either, so you need to use a lot more coals. So, once the lid is back on and sitting on the lifters, pack the coals on it!

I like to cook chicken and turkey up to 175 to 180 degrees Fahrenheit. While that was cooking, I put some coals under my 8-inch oven and started simmering the juices. I added the coconut milk and let it simmer and reduce some. In the end, I added some starch whisked in water to thicken it up as well.

When it was all done, I had also made some rice and heated up some green beans for the full meal. I carved up the chickens and served them. It was moist and not as dry as I thought it would be. It really wasn't an authentic tandoori chicken, as I said, but it was delicious!

BREADED CHICKEN WITH SAUCES

I went through a series of recipes on my blog that involved dredging some chicken breast strips in flour and spices and then frying them. These were accompanied with some kind of sauce, which was baked on like a glaze. I was amazed at the variation of flavors and sauces that were out there! I have included three, but you could certainly find many more!

The first recipe is a sort of Asian-inspired one, with cashews, ginger, soy sauce, and sesame!

CASHEW SESAME CHICKEN

For a picture of this recipe, scan this QR code:

Tools

12-inch dutch oven
20+ coals below for frying
10 coals below for baking
22 coals above

8-inch dutch oven
12+ coals below

Ingredients

2 lbs. boneless and skinless chicken
   breast tenders
1/4 cup flour
1 tsp. black pepper

1 tsp. kosher salt
3 garlic cloves, minced
4 Tbsp. rice wine vinegar
2 Tbsp. brown sugar
1 Tbsp. canola oil
1 tsp. grated fresh ginger
1/2 cup soy sauce
1/4 tsp. red pepper flakes
4 Tbsp. ketchup

1/2 cup cashews
2–3 Tbsp. toasted sesame seeds

1 1/2 cups rice
3 cups water

First, I made sure that the chicken was completely thawed. Then, I lit up about 25–30 coals. When they started to get white, I put about 20 coals under a 12-inch oven. I drizzled two tablespoons of olive oil onto the bottom and let that heat up.

Meanwhile, I mixed the flour, salt, and pepper in a small bowl. If you're using chicken tenders, they're already the right size and shape to bread. If you're using breasts, cut them into strips about one inch thick. I coated the chicken pieces in the flour mixture and put them into the heated, oiled oven. I placed the pieces pretty close together. I Let them fry for 10 minutes on each side, until the chicken was cooked in the middle, and had a nice, brown crust on each side.

I had to fry all the chicken in two batches, because I couldn't get them all into the oven at once.

While the second batch was frying, I came inside and mixed all of the other ingredients in a bowl for the sauce. You can adjust the amounts of everything by taste.

When the second batch of chicken was done, I added those and the first batch into the sauce mix and stirred it, making sure to coat all of the pieces well. I put the oven on top of and underneath the coals to bake all of its contents evenly. I stirred in the cashews and the sesame seeds. At this point, everything was cooked. This step is simply for heating the dish and combining all the flavors.

While this was baking, I put the rice and water into the 8-inch oven and placed this on 12 coals, with the lid on. When I noticed steam venting, I let it cook for about 10 minutes longer and then pulled it off the coals. I let it sit for another 10 to 15 minutes to finish steaming.

Once everything was done, we served the chicken on the rice, and it was delicious!

CHOCOLATE CHICKEN

For a picture of this recipe, scan this QR code:

Chocolate what?

See, it all started when my wife was preparing a lesson for church on Sunday about God's love. She found this funny quote that says, "Chocolate is proof that God loves us all!" While we talked about ways to work that into the lesson (involving a handout with Hershey's Kisses), I had the thought to set aside a day for cooking with chocolate.

I did some research, and I found a great brownie recipe (which is found on page 121), but I wondered what to do for the main dish. I thought about a mole of some kind, and I started looking for recipes. Instead, I found a recipe for a chocolate-based barbecue sauce. Immediately, I thought of the cashew chicken I had done in the previous recipe. I would make the same crispy fried chicken, but I would use chocolate for the sauce!

Though many aspects are the same as with the previous dish, there are a few differences, so I'll start from the top once again.

Tools

12-inch dutch oven

20+ coals below for frying
10 coals below for baking
30+ coals above

8-inch dutch oven
12+ coals below

Ingredients

2 lbs. boneless and skinless chicken
  breast tenders
1/4 cup flour
1 tsp. black pepper
1 tsp. kosher salt
1 tsp. paprika

4 Tbsp. unsalted butter
2–3 cloves garlic, minced
1 small yellow onion, minced
1 (1.5 oz.) chocolate bar, broken
  into chunks
1 (8 oz.) can tomato sauce
1/2 cup sugar
2 tsp. molasses
2 Tbsp. vinegar
2 Tbsp. unsweetened cocoa powder
2 Tbsp. coffee grounds or powdered
  coffee substitute, like Pero
2 Tbsp. dijon mustard
2 tsp. chili powder
2 tsp. kosher salt
1 tsp. ground black pepper

First, I made sure that the chicken was fully thawed before I began.

I started by firing up some coals. Once a few started to turn white, I spread about 20 on the cooking table and put the 12-inch oven on it to preheat, with a few tablespoons of olive oil in the bottom.

While the coals and the dutch oven were getting ready, I prepared the chicken. I mixed the flour and spices in a bowl. I was working with boneless, skinless chicken breasts, so I sliced them into 1-inch strips and dredged them into the flour mix. I set them aside on a plate.

When the oven and the oil were hot, I placed the chicken into the oven to fry. I covered the bottom with about half the chicken, so I had to make it in two batches. I cooked the chicken about 10 minutes on each side. While the first batch was cooking, I chopped the onion and minced the garlic. Once both sides were crispy, and the insides were cooked through, I removed them and put in the second batch. Around this time, I also added fresh coals to the fire to get hot and ready.

While the second batch was cooking, I put the 8-inch oven on the coals and melted the butter. I added the onions and garlic with a little salt. Once the onion slices were translucent, I added the remaining ingredients to melt and simmer.

When the second batch of chicken strips were finished cooking, I pulled the oven off the coals and added the first batch, with the lid on, to keep everything warm with the residual cast iron heat.

When the sauce became nice and smooth, I tasted it and adjusted it. If you find the mix to be a little chocolate-heavy, you can add in more mustard and vinegar. I poured about half of the sauce over the chicken in the oven and stirred it up to coat it over all of the pieces.

Then, I set up the dry bake. I put the 12-inch oven on about 10–12 coals and put a lot of fresh coals (possibly 28–32) on the lid. I lifted the lid and put an old circular grill on the oven as a spacer for the lid. You can see it in the picture.

For a picture of this technique, scan this QR code:

I put the lid back on. In the past I've done that by hooking bent nails over the rim of the dutch oven. With the chicken already cooked, it's just a matter of dry baking the sauce on like a glaze. I let it bake for about another 15 minutes, stirring it once.

Finally, it was ready. I served it with a side of steamed veggies and made brownies for dessert. A chocolate day!

BONELESS BUFFALO CHICKEN

For a picture of this recipe, scan this QR code:

I'm a big fan of hot sauce, and I've always wanted to be able to make it from scratch. I had done some studying a long time ago, and I read about having to store it and let it ferment for months and months. That wasn't going to happen.

Finally, I morphed a bunch I found into this one. It is a great sauce. The amounts are estimates. Really, I just added these things and kept tasting to get it to the point where I liked it. The core ingredients were the butter, the tomato sauce, the heat, and the vinegar.

Tools

12-inch dutch oven
20+ coals below for frying
10 coals below for baking
30+ coals above

8-inch dutch oven
12+ coals below

Chicken
Ingredients

2 lbs. boneless and skinless chicken
   breast tenders
1/4 cup all purpose flour
1 tsp. black pepper
1 tsp. kosher salt
1 tsp. paprika

Sauce
Ingredients

1/2 stick (4 Tbsp.) butter
1/2 onion, minced
2–3 cloves garlic, minced

1 stick (8 Tbsp.) butter
2 (8 oz.) cans tomato sauce
1 Tbsp. cayenne
2–3 Tbsp. vinegar, to taste

1 (4 oz.) can mild green chilies,
   minced
salt
pepper
chili powder or more cayenne to taste

This dish is similar to the sesame cashew chicken and the chocolate chicken in some ways, but in one big way, it is different. I still fried the dredged chicken breast pieces and then made a sauce. Finally I coated them with sauce and baked that on, serving it all up with a little more sauce and side dishes.

In this case, however, since I wanted to give the sauce plenty of time to simmer, I started with it.

I lit up some coals, and once they got white, I put 10–12 of them under my 8-inch dutch oven. I put in the butter to melt. Then I diced and finely minced the onion and the garlic. By this time, the dutch oven was hot and the butter was melted. I tossed in the onion bits and garlic with a little salt and let them sweat.

Once those were translucent, I added in the additional butter, let it melt, and added the tomato sauce, cayenne, and vinegar. These four ingredients (and salt) are really the core of the entire dish. I let it simmer a while and then started tasting it. I added a little more of the cayenne or the vinegar to balance the overall flavor.

Finally, I minced and added the green chilies and the salt and pepper and let it simmer. I used a whisk to briskly stir it and break up the chunks as much as possible.

In between simmerings and tastings, I was also preparing the chicken. This was done just like the other dishes. I first got about 20–24 lit coals under a 12-inch dutch oven, with about 2 tablespoons of olive oil in the bottom.

I mixed up the flour and spices. I sliced the well-thawed chicken breasts (skinless, boneless) into 3–4 short strips each and dredged each chicken piece well in the flour mix. Then, I fried the pieces in the heated 12-inch dutch oven. I had to do it in several batches, because I had more chicken pieces than I could fit into the bottom of the dutch oven. I cooked each piece about 10 minutes a side. I had to pay close attention to the heat under both dutch ovens so that the chicken would brown nicely and the sauce would keep up an easy simmer.

When all of the chicken was done, I put it into the 12-inch dutch oven and drizzled about half the sauce on top. I stirred the chicken and sauce until I could see that each piece was well coated but not soaked. I put about 10 coals under the dutch oven and put a 12-inch circular grill on top of it. Then I put on the lid with upward of 30 coals on it. The grill makes a space under the lid so that moisture can escape. The extra coals on top are needed to make up for the heat that escapes as well. This creates a dry-baking environment, and the sauce cooks onto the chicken in sort of a glaze. There are lots of things you can do to create the gap in the lid. The grill is just one convenient way for me.

I didn't need to bake it long, because everything is actually cooked at that point. I used that extra time to steam a few corn cobs in another 12-inch dutch oven as a side dish.

When I served it up, I included some celery strips and some blue cheese or ranch dressing as an additional sauce to balance out the heat of the cayenne sauce. I was pleased with the results. It was delicious! Unfortunately, the acidic sauce also ate the patina off patches of the bottom of my 8-inch dutch oven, so now I have to reseason it! It was worth it!

ROASTED CORNISH HENS ON BROCCOLI RICE

I was listening to the radio a while back, and I heard a yummy idea. I don't think the people on the radio intended it to be so, because it was a political show, and they were interviewing a restaurant owner in some middle eastern country. The interview was all about how the economy was struggling in the wake of the uprisings in that country—bla, bla, bla, yadda, yadda, yadda . . .

But they had the interview after a meal of roasted dove, which they were eating, as was tradition, with their fingers.

I latched onto the idea. It sounded delicious and a lot of fun to eat. I wanted to do something like that. I pondered it for days. I came up with lots of ideas of different ways to approach it and to make it a full meal, not just a meat dish.

One problem to overcome was the meat. What kind of bird to use? I didn't know where I could get dove. Quail was a possibility. One of the guys in the world championship one year did a great job cooking quail, but they were really small. Then, one day shopping, I found some frozen cornish hens. Perfect! Easy to work with, inexpensive, tasty, and, I think, visually impressive!

This ended up being a simple dish to prepare. Also, for the record, I was not trying to duplicate any particular middle-eastern cuisine or any actual traditional dish. So there is no effort whatsoever to make this authentic. I just made it all up.

Chicken

Tools

12-inch deep dutch oven
10 coals below
12–14 coals above

Ingredients

1 cornish hen for each serving
   (I did 6 and had one left over.)
1 1/2 to 2 cups salt
1/2 cup molasses
about a gallon of water

3 medium onions
salt
pepper
paprika
chili powder

Two days before the meal, I set the little birds (encased in plastic) into the fridge to thaw. Since they're so small, this could probably work in one day, maybe even in the brining process. But I did it over a couple of days.

The morning of the meal, I put about a quart or so of hot tap water into one of my medium stock pots. I put in the salt and the molasses. The hot water helped those to dissolve. Then, I added another quart or so of cold water. I opened up the hen packages and drained them briefly and poked holes in the skin with a knife. A fork works too. I put them in the brined water. I topped off the water just enough to cover the hens and added some ice on top. The ice and the salt should keep the germs at bay, while the meat gets all savory and tender. I set that aside until cooking time later that afternoon.

When the time came, I dumped the brine and set the chickens on cooling racks in the sink to drain. The meat itself will retain a lot of moisture anyway, and I want to minimize the broth at the bottom of the pot.

While the hens were draining, I quartered the onions and scattered them into the bottom of the 12-inch deep dutch oven to hold the hens up above the level of the broth that would cook out.

I patted the hens dry with paper towels and coated them on both sides with liberal shakes of salt, pepper, and paprika and gentle shakes of chili powder. I tucked them into the dutch oven and put them on the coals.

It's a longer, lower-temperature roast. I'm guessing the interior oven temperature is probably around 275 to 300 degrees with the coals numbered above. The cook time was about an hour and a half to two hours. I went for an internal meat temperature of 180 degrees.

Broccoli Rice

Tools

8-inch dutch oven
10–12 coals below

Ingredients

1 1/2 cups rice
3 cups water
juice of 1 lemon
salt
pepper
1 large broccoli head
broth and onions from the
   cornish hens

When the roasting was almost done, I made the rice. It's pretty simple also. I put the rice, water, and lemon juice in the 8-inch dutch oven and put it on the coals with the lid on. While it was coming up to a boil, I cut the broccoli head into tiny florets. I noted when the steam started venting out from under the lid after 10 minutes or so and tossed in the broccoli to steam. I was really quick with the lid, because I didn't want to lose much heat or steam. Maybe 5 minutes later, I pulled the oven off the coals, with the lid still on, to finish cooking.

TORTILLAS

Tools

12-inch dutch oven lid
18–20 coals below

flour tortillas (prepackaged or make your own)

My original idea was to make some tortillas from scratch, and then when we ate, we would pull the meat off with our fingers, put it in a torn tortilla piece along with the rice, and eat it all with our fingers. In the end, I was kinda tired and got lazy, so I used some store-bought tortillas, but even those have to be prepared.

So, I turned a 12-inch dutch oven lid onto a lid stand over several coals and let it get really hot. Then I tossed the tortilla on it and let it heat up and singe a bit. As each one was done, I put it on a plate covered with a tea towel. Hot tortillas are more flexible and tastier.

When it was all done, I pulled the hens out of the dutch oven and spooned onions and broth into the rice, stirring it all up. I put a big spoonful of rice mix on the plate, topped it with the hen, and set out the warm tortillas. We ate them just as I had planned by tearing apart the meat and eating it with the rice in the tortillas. I also set out sour cream and salsa, but it didn't need it much.

It was a lot of fun, both to cook and to eat!

PULLED CHICKEN SANDWICHES

A little while ago, after a stretch of cooking fancier, more challenging dishes, I decided to revisit a traditional dutch oven basic: barbecued chicken. In its simplest form, all you have to do is put some chicken parts in a dutch oven and pour in some barbecue sauce on top of them. Then you roast it up and serve it! No fuss, and a delicious meal. If you have some hamburger buns, you can pull the chicken apart and stir it all back into the sauce and have it as sandwiches.

If you wanted, you could do all that from scratch. Well, I wanted, and this is how I did it.

Buns

(See Sandwich Buns, page 144.)

MARK'S MEAT RUB

Ingredients

1 Tbsp. cumin
1 Tbsp. crushed coriander
1 Tbsp. garlic powder
1 Tbsp. coarse ground black pepper
1 Tbsp. thyme
2 Tbsp. paprika
2 Tbsp. salt
1 tsp. oregano

Chicken

Tools

12-inch shallow dutch oven
10–12 coals below
12–14 coals above

Ingredients

1–2 lbs. boneless, skinless chicken
2 medium onions, quartered
3–4 medium potatoes, cut in 3/4-inch cubes

Sauce

Ingredients

1 (6 oz.) can of tomato paste
1 (8 oz.) can of tomato sauce
brown sugar
mustard
salt
pepper
hot spice (cayenne pepper or chili powder)

To make the buns, see the recipe for Sandwich Buns, in the breads chapter on page 144.

Here's the process for the chicken.

I made sure that the chicken was thawed and patted dry. Then, I coated all of the pieces with the meat rub. I actually had a little left over in a spice jar from another time I used it. It's one of my own spice blends, and I use it a lot.

I cubed up the potatoes and quartered the onions and laid them in the bottom of a dutch oven. I laid the chicken parts above them and set the oven on the coals to roast.

I decided to add the sauce after the fact and let the spice rub flavor the chicken first. I mixed the sauce while the meat was cooking. I didn't put in amounts, because when I make BBQ sauce, I make it more by taste. I started with the cans of tomato paste and sauce, and from there just added each ingredient, tasting along the way. I wanted to get a good balance of all of the ingredients.

When the chicken was cooked to 170 degrees internally, I pulled it off the coals. I put the chicken in a bowl and let them cool a bit, but not too much, just to the point of being cool enough to handle without getting burned. Using a couple of forks, I shredded the chicken.

I also pulled the potatoes and onions out of the dutch oven and separated out the onions as much as I could. I chopped the onions using the mincing knife technique (but still leaving pretty big chunks) and added those back into the chicken. Then, I poured in the sauce and stirred it all together. I didn't use up all of the sauce; just enough to give the chicken a good coating.

The shredded chicken mix is spread in the open sliced buns and served.

The potatoes can be served up as you please. They are tasty as they are, but I actually made a potato salad out of them.

The whole meal was delicious and homey!

CHICKEN ENCHILADA

For a picture of this recipe, scan this QR code:

Let me start off with a quick Spanish lesson. No extra charge!

The word *enchilada* in Spanish has its root in the word *chile*, as in chili pepper. When you add the prefix *en-*, it means to add to or to put on. So, the verb *enchilear* would mean "to put chilies on (or in)." So, if something has been *chilied*, you would say it has been *enchilada*. Thus, the words *pollo enchilada* literally mean "chilied chicken" or "chicken with chilies on it."

The reason I mention this is that there's a common dish in Utah made especially by the non-Hispanics here. It's called a *chicken enchilada*. It involves cooking chicken, wrapping it up with flour tortillas, and covering it with a sauce of sour cream and cream of mushroom soup. Then they put cheese on top of it.

In most cases, it's made without chilies.

So, one might more correctly call it *chicken desenchilada* or *chicken in chile*.

Anyway, in the church ward where I used to live, there was this really sweet lady that had her roots in Mexico. As a part of the ward's annual Relief Society cookbook, she showed this recipe for chicken enchilada. And it's real!

So, I decided to give it a whirl in my dutch oven.

Tools

10-inch dutch oven
8-inch dutch oven
Lots of coals at various points in the process. Once the baking starts, I used 7 on the bottom and 12–13 on the top of the 10-inch oven.

Ingredients

about 1 lb. boneless chicken
about 1/2 lb. grated cheddar

Corn Tortillas

Ingredients

3 Tbsp. flour
3 Tbsp. oil
2 1/2 cups water
6 Tbsp. chili powder (This is where the *enchilada* part comes in.)
1 Tbsp. garlic
salt to taste (probably about 1 Tbsp.)

If I'd had some, I'd have added

1 diced onion
1 small can black olives (diced)

I decided to go as authentic as I could. I started off with the chicken set to boil in the 10-inch dutch oven with the lid on and about 15–18 coals below it.

I put the oil and the flour in the 8-inch oven and set it on coals. In a bowl, I mixed the water, chili powder, garlic, and salt, stirring vigorously to dissolve the chili powder. (It doesn't really dissolve, but if you mix it a lot, it doesn't clump or float and gets well blended with the water).

Once the oil and flour mix was browned, I added the water and chili powder mix and set it to boil. I had to put a lid on top with a few coals.

While that and the chicken boiled, I set to making the tortillas. I got some masa mix and mixed it up, making the dough into balls. I started rolling them between sheets of waxed paper with my rolling pin. Make sure that you mix the tortillas a little moist to make them a little more damp and pliable.

For a griddle, I used an overturned 12-inch lid, with lots of coals underneath. It took a while for it to heat up. You'll want it really hot to cook the tortillas quickly and crispy.

While I was cooking the tortillas, the chicken was fully boiled, so I drained it and put it into a bowl to cool a bit. Also, the sauce in the 8-inch oven bubbled and boiled to the point where it was like a thin gravy. I pulled it off the coals as well. After the chicken had cooled a bit, in between tortilla flips, I shredded the chicken by hand.

The idea is to roll up the chicken in the tortillas. If your tortillas are stiff, you can layer them with the chicken in a sort of lasagna style technique. That's what I did. I started with a base layer of three overlapping tortillas. Over that, I put a layer of shredded chicken. If I'd had the onions and the olives, I would have added a layer of that as well. I also grated in a layer of cheddar. I poured on some of the sauce (again, this is the enchilada part—adding the chilies), covering as much as I could, while still holding back plenty for more layers.

Then, another layer of tortillas, staggered a bit to cover the spots left open by the first layer. More chicken, more cheese, more sauce. Again, had I had olives and onions, there would have been more of those, too.

Finally, after putting on a third layer of tortillas, I poured out the last of the sauce and shredded the last of the cheese onto the top. The lid went on, and it went back on the coals (7 below, 12 or 13 above) for about another 25 minutes.

I have to say, that was a plate of the most kickin' enchiladas I've ever eaten! They rocked. Hot, but not the long-lasting-scorch that often comes in hard-core Mexican. It was zesty and filling and just . . . well . . . wow.

CURRY MINT CHICKEN

For a picture of this recipe, scan this QR code:

I'm honestly not sure where the inspiration for this dish came from. My son, in his culinary classes in high school, had to learn how to carve up a chicken (called *fabricating*) and practice doing it. He had shown me one way to do this about a year ago, but this time, he'd learned a way with some slight variations. He showed me this new way. It was fascinating to learn.

So, of course, as he and I were practicing these skills, we had a bunch of chicken on hand that needed to be used for something, right? Not gonna throw it away, right?

Tools

12-inch shallow dutch oven
10–12 coals below
16–18 coals above

Ingredients

whole chicken, cut up, or about
  3–5 lbs. chicken parts
salt
pepper

1 1/2 to 2 cups plain yogurt
1 Tbsp. curry powder

1 Tbsp. garlic powder
1 tsp. salt
a few shakes chili powder
1/4 cup chopped fresh mint leaves

onions
potatoes

The first step is to prepare the meat. If you're cutting up a whole chicken, that would probably take about a half hour. Since the breasts were the largest pieces of the chicken, I cut each one in half, so that it was about the same size as a thigh. Once it was all cut up into pieces, I made sure they were dry and seasoned each piece with salt and pepper. I set these aside.

If you don't carve up a whole chicken, you can just use packaged breasts, thighs, or other pieces. You can use frozen chicken pieces too, but make sure they're well thawed and patted dry. Then season them and set them aside.

The next step was to mix up the baste. I started with the yogurt. Someday, I'd like to try this with greek-style yogurt, because I really like the texture. I mixed in the curry powder and stirred that in. Different manufacturers make different curry powders. Some are more yellow, others, more red. Some are hot, some are mild and zingy. You can adapt to whatever you've got as long as you taste along the way. Then, I added the other spices and flavorings, stirring and tasting as I went.

Decide in advance how hot you want the result to be and shoot for that level with the chili powder. Be cautious with it. Add a little, taste, and add a little more, etc. Be aware that the yogurt will cool the capsaicin a little, so the heat will come on as an aftertaste.

Finally, be liberal with the mint. Mint adds a rich coolness to the tang of the yogurt and the spice of the curry and chilli powder.

I went out and lit up the coals. While they were starting to glow, I chopped up the onions and potatoes into 1-inch-sized chunks and tossed them together into the dutch oven. They are delicious and will lift the chicken up out of the juices that will gather at the bottom.

The last step is to layer the chicken pieces over the onions and potatoes, and thickly slather the yogurt mix over the top of the chicken. Close up the lid, add the coals above and below, and begin baking.

I cooked them until they were at an internal temperature of about 175 degrees. Chicken is actually safe to eat at around 160^0, but if you cook it longer, it falls off the bone more and is more done. It won't dry out in a dutch oven, because the heavy lid traps the moisture. It took about 40–50 minutes for it to be done. About halfway, I put on more baste.

In the end, it was delicious! The leftovers the next day were even more flavorful, since the herbs absorbed deeper into the yogurt.

CHAPTER 3

NOTHING AGAINST MY VEGAN AND VEGETARIAN FRIENDS, but I really like the taste of beef. I like all kinds of meat when prepared right, even esoteric things like squid, eel, or duck. Beef, however, is wonderful. When cooked right, it has a delectable juiciness and earthy flavor that can't be substituted.

It's also one of those meats that can be found in a haute cuisine dish, like a beef wellington or a low-brow favorite like a burger.

There are cows and variants of cows all over the world, making some form of beef into one of the foods that unites us as a world culture, much like rice.

Beef is also perfect for slow-roasting in cast iron. It's a rich and juicy way to cook beef. Here are my favorite beef recipes.

RUBBED ROAST

For a picture of this recipe, scan this QR code:

One Sunday, as I was contemplating what to cook, I was tempted by a beef roast we had in the freezer. I wondered how to do it, and my wife suggested that I do the traditional onion soup mix braise. This is a common way to prepare a pot roast in a slow roaster (Crock Pot) where you sprinkle a commercial onion soup seasoning mix onto the beef in the slow cooker, toss in the potatoes, carrots, etc., and add some water and cook it for a few hours. That got me thinking! I looked up the ingredients of the mix and thought of my own ideas. I came up with what would become my roast rub!

It turned out, sadly, that I was way low on veggies, so I ended up only adding in carrots, but it was still delicious and tender. When you do this, you can put in many more veggies and build the flavors.

Tools

12-inch dutch oven
20–24 coals below for browning/searing
12 coals below for roasting
12–14 coals above

Ingredients

4–6 lbs. beef roast

Rub

I don't include amounts here, because I just sprinkled and scattered the ingredients over the top of the roast and flipped it and did the same to the bottom.

Ingredients

dried onion chips
dried green and red pepper
garlic powder
salt
pepper
chili powder
parsley
olive oil

Extra veggies in the pot

(all optional)

1 cup baby carrots or 2 peeled and
    sliced carrots
2–3 celery stalks, chopped
2–3 medium yellow onions,
    quartered or sliced
2–3 medium potatoes, cubed

Gravy

Ingredients

1 heaping Tbsp. flour
1/2 cup hot water
lemon juice

Remember to start with a fully thawed roast. A couple of days in the fridge or a few hours under cool water will do the trick. Once it was thawed, I put it on a plate and sprinkled, grated, and tossed the rub ingredients onto it. I was liberal with the garlic powder and the dried onions and peppers, but cautious with the chili powder. (It's homemade and has a big, bad kick.) I drizzled on the olive oil and rubbed it into the surface of the meat. Then, I flipped it over and did the same to the other side.

I let that sit, covered with plastic, on the counter while I got the coals and the dutch oven ready. That allowed the seasonings to absorb more fully into the meat, especially the salt (which also tenderizes).

While that was getting more and more flavorful, I got some coals lit and put a lot of coals under my 12-inch, with a bit of olive oil in the bottom. I let it sit and heat up.

Finally, I could tell it was really hot, and I put the meat on the bottom of the open dutch oven. Immediately it started sizzling, showing me that my waiting was worth it!

After a few minutes, I turned it over and I could see the sear on the meat and the blackening of the spice rub. The smell was wonderful! By the way, searing the meat does not seal in the juices. It triggers what's called the Maillard reaction, which browns the surface of the meat and gives it that sweetish tangy tones that we love so much!

Once the second side was seared, I rearranged the coals for roasting. (I also replenished a bit, since they were starting to diminish.) Every 20–25 minutes or so, I would take coals from my chimney and replenish them under my dutch oven and on the lid. Then, I'd add more fresh ones to the chimney to start. I think, in the end, I cooked it about 2 1/2 to 3 hours. When I was about an hour away from serving, I started getting the veggies ready. In this case, that just involved checking the fridge to see what was available and opening up a bag of baby carrots into the dutch oven. If I'd had potatoes, onions, or anything else, I would have cut them up and added them to the dutch oven around the meat.

Finally, it was done. I brought it in and removed the meat and veggies to a serving plate. Then, I took the gravy ingredients and the dutch oven back out to the coals. First, I dribbled in some lemon juice (2 tablespoons or more), and used that acid with the heat to scrape up all of the yummy brown fond that the meat had left on the bottom. Then, I whisked together the water and the flour (so there were no clumps), and slowly whisked it into the liquid in the dutch oven. It heated and boiled and became a wonderful gravy.

The meat was tender and flavorful, the veggies were perfect, and the gravy livened them all up and tied them together. It was a delicious meal.

ABSOLUTELY AMAZING DUTCH OVEN BURGERS

For a picture of this recipe, scan this QR code:

One day, I was browsin' the web when I came across this recipe for black bean burgers. I was intrigued, because even though I'm not usually interested when a vegetable pretends to be meat, this recipe actually looked pretty good. I'll probably try it sometime soon.

However . . .

On this particular day, I decided I wanted to do it with meat, because it looked so amazing.

I had decided that it would be an excellent chance for me to practice grilling under my wonderful new gazebo, but after prepping all the meat and the fixings, I discovered that "someone" had forgotten to close the valve on the propane cylinder the last time we used it, and we were out of gas. Seriously, I don't know who could have done such a thing. I find it unconscionable and almost unforgivable. But, we must move on.

At that point, I decided to go ahead and cook them dutch oven style and fired up some coals.

Tools

12-inch shallow dutch oven
22+ coals underneath

lid of a 12-inch dutch oven
22+ coals underneath

Toppings
(All optional)

lettuce
tomatoes
onions
pickles
cooked bacon
mayo
ketchup
mustard

Burger Meat
Ingredients

2+ lbs. ground beef
1 onion (grated)
4–5 cloves garlic, minced
salt
pepper
cumin
chili powder
paprika
a handful of fresh parsley

kaiser rolls (Alternately, you can bake your own buns using the recipe in the breads chapter on page 144.)
butter

sliced cheese (I used sharp cheddar)

The first step was to mix up the meat. This was simple, and I mixed the ingredients for the meat all together. I actually chose the spices based on my own whims rather than on the recipe I found. Each one was about a teaspoon, except for the chili powder, which was only a few sprinkles. My homemade chili powder is pretty strong. You can adjust yours to your own powders and tastes.

I also sliced the topping onions, the tomatoes, and the cheese.

I put the dutch oven on the coals and let it preheat for quite a while. I really wanted it to be really hot at first. I made my patties fairly large, partly because I knew they'd have to fit on a kaiser roll, and also because I knew they'd shrink as they cooked. By the way, I chose the kaiser rolls because they are a bit firmer than typical store-bought hamburger buns. Those things are pathetic. I also made larger patties, 'cause I'm a guy, and I like to have lots of meat on my burgers. I know it's not healthy, but once in a while, ya gotta live large.

I put the patties in the dutch oven and used it as a griddle. Because it was so hot to start with, it got a pretty good sear on the first side.

While the first round of patties were cooking, I got more coals under an inverted dutch oven lid (on a trivet-stand) and let it heat up. After turning the burgers, I brushed butter on the inside of the kaiser rolls and put them on the heated lid to toast, butter-side down. After the meat turns once and is cooked a bit, it's a good time to put on the cheese so it can melt.

I was careful not to overcook the burgers. I did cook them all the way through but not dry. It's tricky to get to that, I think. But, it worked that night. I think the dutch oven is not as hot as most gas grills, which helped me to not dry them out. I also think it's very important for burgers to be topped and served the instant they come off the heat. The longer you wait, the drier and crustier they get. Not good. If you're serving family, have them gather and bless the food after you do the first flip, or it will be too late.

Finally, I pulled the buns off the lid (griddle), put the burger, sizzling, onto the bun, and let the family top it as they pleased. For my money, I love lots of extra stuff on my burgers, so I tend to layer it pretty high. Even with the additional flavors, the spices and the flavor of the meat came through. It was possibly the best burgers I've ever made.

LONG-ROASTED BEEF BRISKET

For a picture of this recipe, scan this QR code:

When I first tried this dish, I'd been wanting to for possibly as long as a year. As I would shop, I'd go past the meat counter and see these huge slabs of brisket meat, and I'd think, "That would be so much fun to cook up." I had this idea of doing one and inviting the entire neighborhood over for a pot luck.

Well, finally one weekend, I had the chance! We were at a campground at Bear Lake with a group of families with children with special medical needs. The group is called "Hope Kids," and we've got many wonderful friends in it.

So, for dinner Saturday night, I cooked this brisket. It was about 11+ pounds, and at a rate of about a half hour per pound, that meant a good six-hour cook time. I started at about noon.

Tools

14-inch deep dutch oven
14–16 coals below
16–20 coals above

Ingredients

1 beef brisket, anywhere from
8–12 lbs. (figure about 1/2 lb.
per person)

Mark's Meat Rub

1 Tbsp. cumin
1 Tbsp. crushed coriander
1 Tbsp. garlic powder
1 Tbsp. coarse ground black pepper
1 Tbsp. thyme
2 Tbsp. paprika
2 Tbsp. salt
1 tsp. oregano
and I added some chili powder
    this time

Sauce

1 (6 oz.) can of tomato paste
1 (8 oz.) can of tomato sauce
brown sugar (or regular sugar and
    molasses)
mustard
salt
pepper
some kind of hot spice (cayenne
    pepper or chili powder)

I started out by opening up the brisket and sprinkling it with the meat rub (which I mixed the night before) on both sides. I rubbed it in a bit. I let it sit for a while and lit up about 35 coals or so.

I lightly oiled the inside of my 14-inch deep dutch oven. Usually, when I do a roast, I'll put in a layer of quartered onions and potato chunks for that purpose, but with a six-hour cook time, they would be mush by the end of it. In the end, I decided that the brisket would fit better if I just put it on the bottom and draped it up the sides.

With the meat in place, I put it on the coals. I stuck in a thermometer, mostly to monitor progress. It will cook way past done.

This is the kind of cooking that I especially like. I can sit back and relax with a soda and watch the coals burn. About every 20–30 minutes, I'd pull a few coals out of the chimney and replenish them on the oven. I'd usually put about four around the bottom and six or so on top. Then, I'd add more fresh coals to the pile to light up. While I was doing this, friends and families that were camping with us would come by and chat. I got to meet a few people who are dutch oven chefs, and a few who'd actually bought my books.

After about 2 1/2 hours, the meat was at a medium doneness. It hit well done probably an hour and a half later. I just kept on cooking and rotating the coals. At about four o'clock, I started to work on another 14-inch pot of au gratin potatoes, a great side dish for this main.

Finally, about an hour before serving time, I mixed up the BBQ sauce. When I mix this up, I make it like a good jazz tune, with lots of improvisation. I start with a core of the tomato, the mustard, and the sugar (or, in this case, the molasses), and then I keep adding flavors and things one at a time until it all balances. Too sweet? Too tomatoey? Add more mustard. Too tangy? More sugar and molasses. Not enough edge? More black pepper and chili powder . . . and always just enough salt to make it come alive. I basted it over the visible surface of the brisket and let it bake on. I did this two or three times, and I reserved the remaining sauce to drizzle over the dish as it was served.

When it was all done and time to eat, I cut the brisket in half and put half on my cutting board. I cut thin slices against the meat's grain and served it with a drizzle of additional BBQ sauce. It was so juicy, tender, and delicious. The sauce and the rub really added to the overall flavor. I was proud of it. I want to do this again and again!

CARNE ASADA

I've always loved the taste of carne asada, and I've wanted to do it for a long time. When I finally decided to do it, I kept thinking of more and more things to add to the meal. In the end, I did an elaborate Mexican-inspired meal, but the carne asada was just a part of it all. It was interesting juggling the various pots to make all of the elements of the meal, as well as timing them all to be done right. For this book, I'll just add the recipe for the Carne.

Tools

12-inch dutch oven
25+ coals below

Meat

Ingredients

2–3 lbs. thinly sliced beef steaks
juice of three limes
salt
pepper
paprika
cumin
4–6 cloves garlic

Salsa

Ingredients

3–4 tomatoes
3 medium onions
2 green peppers
1–2 jalapenos
juice of 2 limes
salt
paprika
olive oil
fresh cilantro

Serve with

flour or corn tortillas
sour cream
guacamole
cheese

I started in the morning and put all of the meat ingredients into a zip-top bag and shook it to evenly coat the steaks with the marinade. I put the bag into the fridge and went to church.

Later that afternoon, I lit up some coals, and while they were heating up, I prepared the veggies in the salsa. I cut the tomatoes and the onions into wedges, like in sixths or eighths. The peppers I simply sliced into long sticks, like a big julienne.

I put a lot (about 25+) of fresh coals under my 12-inch oven and drizzled some olive oil in the bottom to heat up. Once that was heated, I started with the veggies. I started with just the tomatoes, because everything has different cooking times. I put the wedges in, skin down. Immediately, it started sizzling. I didn't stir it. The idea is to get a good sear going to caramelize it. I kept the lid off for this process. It's okay to soften the tomato flesh a bit too.

Once the tomatoes were all seared, I pulled them out and set them aside and let the heat build back up. Then, I did the same thing with the peppers, onions, and jalapenos. I laid the onions on their sides instead on the back of the wedges.

Once they were all seared and cooked (but not sautéd), I put them all on my chopping block and chopped them into coarse chunks. The tomatoes, of course, sort of fell apart and provided a richness that I hadn't found in normal pico de gallo. It was delicious!

I got some fresh coals under the dutch oven again and heated it up. I wanted it good and hot, so I used new coals, not the half-burned ones that were left. I spread out two pieces of the meat and let it sear and sizzle only a few minutes on each side so that it still had a thin sliver of pink in the middle. When each one was done, I brought them in. I cut them into long, thin slices, and we served them with the salsa in tortillas, with guacamole and sour cream. I also made rice and refried beans (from scratch) for side dishes. All in all, it was a delicious Mexican meal!

BEEF AND BRUSSELS

For a picture of this recipe, scan this QR code:

One thing I've enjoyed a lot in my cooking is to challenge myself to take an ingredient or a dish that I hated as a kid and see if I can do it well enough to say, "I like it!" In this dish, I tackle brussels sprouts!

Like all the others (asparagus, broccoli, etc.), I didn't dive in without some research. I got a lot of ideas. This would be a momentous occasion. I didn't want it to be a simple side dish. I thought about various meats that would help make it a main dish, and In the end, I thought that the bitter tones of the sprouts would go best paired with beef. Many of the recipes I checked out included bacon as well, and I liked that combination. So, I stuck with that as well. Portobello mushrooms are beefy also, so that was an obvious ingredient to add as well.

I found a lot of ways to cook them. Most of my friends and my research warned against overcooking them. In the end, I decided to do it as a stir fry.

Tools

12-inch dutch oven
24–28 coals underneath

Ingredients

1/2 lb. bacon, chopped
1 lb. fresh brussels sprouts
1 lb. beef, in steak or cubed/sliced as stir fry

1 medium onion
1 green pepper
1 large portobello mushroom
2–3 cloves garlic
salt
pepper
paprika
oregano

Gorgonzola cheese

This was actually a pretty easy one to do. I started by lighting the coals. When they were hot, I put them underneath the dutch oven and put the bacon pieces into it. I wanted to cook them until they were really crispy.

While that was cooking, I prepared the meat and the veggies. I sliced the meat up first and sprinkled it with salt, pepper, and paprika. I let it sit while I sliced, chopped, and minced everything else. Finally, it all went into the same bowl, and I gave it a few shakes.

I let the bacon cook pretty crisp and then pulled it out. I amped up the coals and let the drippings get really hot. I tossed in the meat and veggies. I gave it a stir right away. I would alternate stirring with letting the beef and the veggies sear. I cooked it all until the meat was medium and the veggies were slightly soft. Then I pulled it off the coals.

I served it with some sprinkles of the Gorgonzola on top, alongside some roasted potato chunks I'd done in a 10-inch oven. Wow. It was all delicious! Another childhood terror conquered!

Next? Probably squash . . .

MARK'S ROLLED STEAK ROAST

For a picture of this recipe, scan this QR code:

This was an experiment I tried a few weeks ago. I'd seen things like it in pictures and magazines, and I'd seen something pre-prepared in my grocer's meat section. I'd thought about how to do it myself and wasn't sure if I could pull it off.

The idea is to get some thin steaks and roll some delicious veggies inside them, almost like a beef sushi. Except, of course, that you cook it and the green stuff is on the inside. Okay, it's really nothing like a sushi.

I think it ended up quite tasty, and elegant as well.

Tools

12-inch shallow dutch oven
10–12 coals below
12–14 coals above

Ingredients

2 lbs. steak cut in 1/4-inch thickness or less
salt
pepper
paprika
cayenne
thyme
sage
parsley
garlic
fresh baby spinach
asparagus
provolone cheese
5–6 potatoes, cubed
2 onions, quartered

I started out by lighting a bunch of coals and letting them get white.

Meanwhile, I seasoned both sides of the steaks by shaking on the herbs and spices you see listed. I don't list amounts, because I just went with what I grabbed first and estimated what might be good. You may end up with totally different spices when you go to your cabinet. Balance them with a bit of care, however. Be gentle with the cayenne, for example. You want it to have some kick but not burn. Once the meat was seasoned, I set it aside for a while.

In the meantime, I minced the garlic and cut the stems off the baby spinach. I also snapped the ends off the asparagus and cut up the potatoes and onions.

About this time, the coals were ready. I spread some oil around the inside and put a tablespoon or two of olive oil in the bottom. I set this on and under the coals to preheat. This will also set some of the oil and help build up your patina.

Then, to rolling the meat.

I laid out the strips of meat side-by-side with the seasoned face down so that the edges were overlapping a little. I scattered the minced garlic over the upside and laid out the spinach leaves in a pattern about 2–3 leaves thick to cover the meat. On top of that, I spread a layer of thinly sliced provolone. Finally, across the bottom, I took the asparagus sprigs and laid them out, alternating them to get the heads of the stalks in different places along the meat so that when I sliced it, it would evenly be distributed.

Finally, I rolled it all up tightly.

I tied it with some string. It's tricky to describe how I tied it. I slid the string underneath at one end and tied a knot. Then I slid more string, starting from the other end, until it was a few inches from the first knot. I looped it under itself and tightened it. I kept repeating this step until the entire roll was secure. I drizzled on a little more olive oil.

Cooking it was a little tricky. I poured the potatoes and onions into the now-heated dutch oven and spread them out. I tossed in a little bit of salt and pepper, just for good measure. I laid the steak roll over the potatoes and stuck in a short-stemmed thermometer before closing the lid.

I cooked it to an internal temperature of about 145. Since the steak is thin and the thermometer is essentially sticking into the veggies, it's a good gauge, but not fully accurate to the steak's doneness. That was good, but subsequently, I cooked it much longer to let the meat get to a more fall-apart doneness and to get the heat into the veggies inside.

When it's done, pull it off the coals, but let it rest while you set the table. Then, slice it into medallions or sushi slices, or whatever you want to call them, and serve them on their side with the potatoes and onions and whatever other side dishes you've also made. It's really an elegant presentation!

CHAPTER 4

PORK, GAME MEAT, AND FISH

WHEN I COOK A WHITE MEAT, I'm usually cooking chicken, but I really love pork as well, in all its forms. It's different than chicken and cooks in a different way. It can be tricky to cook pork without drying it. Using a lower temperature and a slower cook time will typically help with that.

I also love cooking game meats, and I'm a big seafood fan as well!

JAZZY BBQ PORK RIBS WITH POTATOES

For a picture of this recipe, scan this QR code:

I've not done a lot of ribs over the years, but I have done some. I've done enough to learn three things that are important keys to yummy, fall-off-the-bones, mess-all-over-your-fingers-and-face dutch oven ribs.

First, a good spice rub. This lays the foundation of seasoning and flavor for your ribs. Gotta have it.

Second, a good barbecue sauce. This is the second layer. There are as many ways to make a good sauce as there are people cooking, so you really have to try to go wrong. Each sauce brings its own nuances and subtleties. Tangy? Sweet? Sticky? Sloppy? Hot? Fruity? You can adjust it to your heart's content.

And finally, a long cook time. Cooking the ribs until they're at the government-recommended temperature for doneness and safety isn't gonna cut it. Yeah, it'll taste good, but you'll have to gnaw it all off the bone instead of just letting it fall off. You've got to cook it well past done to get to that point. Fortunately, doing that in a dutch oven won't dry out the meat, because the moisture will be trapped under the heavy lid.

One other thing I have to say about this (and I've mentioned this in other recipes in this book) is that sometimes cooking is like playing classical music. I pay really close attention to the recipe, and I measure out the spices and ingredients as if I were reading the music note-for-note. Other times, a great meal should be like a good jazz tune. You have a lead sheet with the melody and the chord structure, but it's not so much notes as it is guidelines. You really make it up as you go, and you never play the same song the same way twice.

Tools

12-inch deep dutch oven
12 coals below
14–16 coals above

Ingredients

1 rack of pork baby back ribs

Mark's Meat Rub

1 Tbsp. cumin
1 Tbsp. crushed coriander
1 Tbsp. garlic powder
1 Tbsp. coarse ground black pepper
1 Tbsp. thyme
2 Tbsp. paprika
2 Tbsp. salt
1 tsp. oregano
and I added some chili powder this time

3–4 medium potatoes, cubed
2–3 medium onions, cut into eighths

Mark's Awesome Sauce

Ingredients

1 (6 oz.) can of tomato paste
1 (8 oz.) can of tomato sauce
brown sugar (or regular sugar and molasses)
mustard
something acidic, like lemon juice or balsamic vinegar
salt
pepper
some kind of hot spice (cayenne pepper or chili powder)

As I said, this is more improvised jazz than it is formalized classical. The recipes above are for my traditional spice rub and my own barbecue sauce. One time, when I was out of the spice rub and was feeling a bit minimal, I just went back to basics: salt, black pepper, paprika, garlic powder, and just a bit of chili powder. All of the other flavors are great too. Just do what you want!

I opened the ribs package and cut them into chunks of about four ribs each. That's the only way you'll get them into the dutch oven. I rubbed the spices over the surfaces (both sides), covered them with plastic wrap, and put them in a baking pan in the fridge. While that was chilling and soaking in the flavors, I lit up the coals.

I lightly oiled the inside of the dutch oven. I don't know that it was really necessary, but I did it anyway. A lot of the fat from the ribs will render out, so you probably don't need to oil the inside of the oven unless you want to. Then I set the rib chunks in however I could get them. You could probably fit them into a regular dutch oven, but when you add the potatoes and onions later, you'll want it deeper.

I covered the dutch oven and set it on and under the coals. It was a windy day, so I had to keep the side fire going and add more coals to the oven about every 15–20 minutes. I had planned on about a three-hour cook time. Occasionally, I would check on the ribs, but not very often.

After about two hours, I started preparing the rest of the items. I made the barbecue sauce first. This, also, was improvised. One day, I used molasses instead of sugar, and balsamic vinegar as well as mustard and lemon juice for the acid. It gave it a dark look and great tanginess. If you like yours sweeter, use more sugar or some fruit preserves. For more heat, add more chili powder or tabasco. Add, stir, taste.

I cubed up the potatoes and the onions. In retrospect, some sliced or diced green or red peppers would have been nice to add as well.

Out at the dutch oven, I pulled the ribs out and tossed in the potatoes and onions. I stirred them to mix them and break up the onions a little. Then I restacked the ribs on top of the potatoes. With a silicon basting brush, I coated one side of the meat with a thick, liberal layer of sauce. Using tongs, I flipped them over and coated the other side.

I put the lid back on and replenished the coals. After about another 15–20 minutes, I opened it up again and could see the sauce baking onto the ribs. It really looked great. I slathered on another layer of sauce, turned them over, and did the same to the other side. I drizzled more sauce over the onions and potatoes too. I closed it up and replenished the heat again. Finally, by the third time, I could see that they were about ready. I pulled it all in, and we set the table. Just before serving, I put another coat of sauce on.

The rendered fat from the ribs had done a nice job browning and crisping the potatoes, and the bold flavors of the rub and the sauce on the ribs was amazing. It just doesn't get better!

PORK LOIN MEDALLIONS

For a picture of this recipe, scan this QR code:

Sometimes, I get so busy doing signings, appearances, and demos for my books that I forget how much fun it is to just cook for the family. When I worked up this meal, I'd forgotten how much I enjoy looking forward to trying something new that I've never done before. It had truly been a long time.

So, I kinda went overboard.

My sister-in-law had given us a frozen pork loin, and I'd been going over in my head what I could do with it. I finally came up with this idea, and when we had to cancel on a birthday party because of car troubles, I jumped at the chance.

But my dear wife asked if I could make some au gratin potatoes and some dinner rolls. I thought it would be cool to round out the meal with a dessert—like brownies.

I ended up doing all four dishes in my dutch ovens. It was kinda hectic, but the results were worth it. Yummy to the core! The potatoes and the brownies already have their recipes enshrined in the Black Pot Blog, but the rolls and the pork loin do not. Here is the latter first.

Tools

12-inch shallow dutch oven
20–24 coals underneath

Ingredients

1 pork loin
1 lb. bacon

juice of 1 lemon
1/4 cup water
1 heaping Tbsp. flour

liberal shakes of
  salt
  pepper
  paprika
  thyme
  basil

This recipe doesn't have much to it. It's simple, and the cool thing is that it looks impressive. Start early in the day by getting the loin thawed under cool water.

I actually made this dish late in the day. I cooked and baked all the other dishes first, because this one takes the least amount of time, and it's the most critical to be served fresh. First, make sure you have some fresh coals lit.

I mixed up generous amounts of each of the spices. I kept tasting the mix with my fingertip until it seemed like the right blend. You can actually use whatever seasonings and herbs you want. This combination turned out really good. I just mixed it in a small bowl.

The loin came out of the package in two halves. I cut each one into quarters, which were about 2- to 2 1/2-inches long. Then I butterflied each piece. To butterfly, slice the piece in half against the grain, but don't cut all the way through. (Almost all the way through, but not completely.) Then, open the slice up like a book and you have a disc of meat. I lightly dredged the top and the bottom in the seasoning mix. Then I took a single strip of bacon and wrapped it around the side, securing it with a couple of toothpicks. I continued until all the meat was butterflied, seasoned, and wrapped. While it was absorbing the seasonings, I got the oven ready.

I spread out some coals and set my 12-inch oven on them. I sprinkled a little olive oil in the bottom and let it get all shimmery hot. Then, I gently laid each wrapped medallion on the hot oven bottom. After 5–10 minutes, I turned them over and let them cook/sear on the other side. About this time, I put the lid on so that the internal heat would cook the meat all the way through. This, however, is not strictly necessary.

When they were cooked through, I pulled them off and put them on a plate tented in aluminum foil. I squeezed the lemon juice into the bottom of the pan and scraped loose the fond pieces. There was liquid from the pork in the bottom as well, so that helped. I added the flour to the water and stirred it thoroughly. I added it to the pot to thicken and smooth the juices into a sauce.

In the end, I served the medallions up with the potatoes and the rolls, drizzled with just a hint of sauce. It was truly elegant and delicious!

DUTCH OVEN HAM

For a picture of this recipe, scan this QR code:

From My Blog

"Yesterday, I had another one of those dutch oven cooking days where everything went right. It was truly a five-star meal, or at least four stars!

"The centerpiece of the meal was a dutch oven ham recipe that was actually done pretty simply, with just a few ingredients. Basically, it's a honey and brown sugar glaze. I'd seen some recipes that used this particular approach, but I took it in a slightly different direction.

"At first, I thought I'd flavor it up a bit with maybe some apple juice or dried apples and cinnamon and nutmeg. But then I decided that was too obvious and I should shake things up a bit. So, I ended up going with a chili powder in the mix.

"That worked really well, because you get this three-layered flavor thing happening. When you bite into it, especially a cut with a glazed edge, you get the sweet sugar first, and a few moments later, a bit of heat. Finally the salt of the ham meat itself came through.

Tools

Deep dutch oven, 12- or 14-inch, depending on the size of your ham
12-inch: 25–28 coals, split evenly between above and below
14-inch: 30–33 coals, split evenly between above and below

Ingredients

2 cups brown sugar
2 Tbsp. salt
1+ Tbsp. pepper

1–2 tsp. chili powder
1 uncooked ham, thawed
3–6 ounces honey

"Not much to it, is there? I kept thinking, *Wait, this is too simple. What else should I put in there?* But I couldn't think of anything else it needed that would enhance it. Simple is good, it seems, especially in ham recipes.

"I started off making the rub. This is also simple. I mixed the ingredients into a small bowl and stirred them together with a fork. Now, your chili powder my be weaker or stronger than mine, so taste the mix and see how it balances. Then you can adjust the pepper and the chili so it's there but not too strong.

"The amount of the rub used will depend a lot on the size of your ham. I actually ended up doubling this one because I was baking a 10 pound ham. Use these same approximate proportions and just make it to your taste.

"Put the ham in the dutch oven and make sure that you can close the lid over it. Depending on the size and shape, you might have to position it differently, or, as I did yesterday, have to cut a chunk off. I have honey in one of those squeeze bottles, so I drizzled it all over the ham. Using a basting brush, I spread it out, especially on the sides.

"Then I took the rub and smeared it all over the ham, letting it adhere to the sides with the honey. I let that sit for ten to 20 minutes and absorb into the meat a bit.

"I put it on the coals, and from that point on, it was simply a matter of managing the heat from the coals and occasionally using a baster to pick up the juicy syrup and re-spread it onto the ham. I also had some sugar mix left over, so after a couple of hours, I also dusted that back on top for some more glazing.

"It cooked for about three hours total, to an internal temperature of 160 or so. At that point I took it off the coals and brought it in to the table. By the time we were all gathered, it had risen up to about 170.

"My family pronounced this dutch oven ham recipe delicious!"

DUTCH OVEN PORK CHOPS WITH DRESSING AND GLAZE

Another Delicious Blog Entry

"We had a whole bunch of friends coming over one Sunday night. Not being sure what to cook initially, we settled on pork chops, since that's what we had. I did some digging around and found some good recipes. This is what I chose.

54   MARK HANSEN

Tools

12-inch dutch oven
18 coals above
9 coals below

Dressing
Tools and Ingredients

8-inch dutch oven
10–12 coals below

2 medium onions, diced
3 stalks celery, diced
1 cube butter, sliced (to mix more
  evenly)
5–6 slices of bread, diced (I used
  sourdough rye)

Glaze
Ingredients

4 oranges, juice and zest
1/2 cup orange or pineapple juice
1 1/2 cup sugar
1 tsp. ground cinnamon

Meat
Ingredients

4–6 pork chops
salt and pepper to taste

1 large apple, cored, peeled, and
  diced
1/4 cup slivered almonds
2 Tbsp. parsley flakes
1 tsp. rosemary
1 tsp. paprika
1 tsp. allspice
2 tsp. salt
2 tsp. fresh ground black pepper
1/2 cup water

1 tsp. salt
10 whole cloves
2–3 Tbsp. cornstarch

"I started by mixing all the dressing ingredients together in a bowl. Then I put the dressing evenly on the bottom of the dutch oven. I rubbed the pork chops with liberal shakes of salt and coarse ground pepper and arranged them above the dressing. (You can use commercial steak seasoning if you want to.) It's okay to overlap some if you have to. Then I put the oven on the coals. Because bread was on the bottom, I turned the oven frequently to avoid hot spots.

"While that was cooking, I prepared the glaze. I shaved the zest off the orange skin and chopped it up to be a bit finer. That went right into the 8-inch dutch oven. I juiced the oranges right into the dutch oven too. That was all the original recipe called for. But it looked like not enough liquid since I had squeezed the juice with my bare hands, not a juicer. So, I added the pineapple juice. Then I added all the other glaze ingredients, except the cornstarch. That also went on some coals right away. I quickly got it boiling, and I adjusted the coals to a steady simmer.

"Once it was boiling, I took the lid off to help it boil down and thicken. I added the cornstarch a little at a time, waiting between each application to see how thick it was getting.

"The pork chops cooked about 45 minutes to an hour, and by that time, the glaze was nice and thick. I pulled it off the coals. Then I scooped up the dressing that's under the pork chops and served them together with some glaze poured over the top. It was delicious!"

DR. PEPPER HAM

A tradition in many church congregations is the dinner group. The basic idea is that everyone who wants to signs up, and each family is assigned to a group, usually of three to five total families. They get together for dinner once a month, rotating the household that hosts each time, until everyone has had a turn and they've all gotten to know each other.

Then everyone is shuffled up and it starts over again.

Fellowship over food.

So, one night it was our turn to host. I immediately thought about cooking up a meal in my dutch oven so I could show off my mad dutchin' skillz—I mean, humbly serve my fellow man, of course.

But what to cook that would do both?

The previous Easter I'd done a big ham in a Dr Pepper sauce, and I wanted to try it again. I looked through my records and the Internet and I couldn't find the recipe. I did, however, find another one for Pork Ribs. I thought I could modify it for the ham, so I did.

Tools

14-inch dutch oven
15–17 briquettes each, above and
   below

Ingredients

10 lbs. ham shank
1 yellow bell pepper, diced
1 large tomato, diced
1 large onion, diced
1 (20 oz.) can pineapple chunks
1 (11 oz.) can mandarin oranges
20–24 oz. Dr Pepper (2 cans, 1
   bottle, etc.) Not diet.
1 cup mild to medium commercial
   salsa
1 cup brown sugar
3 Tbsp. minced garlic
salt and pepper (lots of coarse,
   ground pepper for my taste)

I started by thawing the ham overnight in the fridge. The next day, I started cooking it at around three o'clock.

When it was time, I opened and drained the package and put the ham into the dutch oven and cut half-inch scores crisscrossed over the top of the meat about two inches apart. Then I added the pepper, the tomato, and the onion. I drained the syrup of the canned fruits into a bowl and dumped the pineapples and oranges into the oven also.

I mixed the fruit syrups, the Dr Pepper, the salsa, the brown sugar, and the garlic in the bowl and poured the mixture into the dutch oven. I suppose you could dump it all into the oven at once, but the Dr Pepper helps dissolve the sugar.

"Then I put it on the heat. I cooked the ham for about three hours. Every half hour I'd open it up and use a ladle to pour the juice, veggies, and fruits on top of the ham. About every hour I'd refresh the coals. If you use this recipe, be sure you've got your side fire goin' on.

When it was all done, I carved the ham from the oven and served the slices on a plate. In a separate bowl, I used a straining spoon to pull up the veggies and fruits as a sweet/salty side dish.

Everyone was thrilled with the meal. One family brought a salad, another brought dessert, and we all had a great time. And what a spread!

THANKSGIVING TURKEY AND HAM IN THE DUTCH OVENS

For a picture of this recipe, scan this QR code:

This is a continuation of the Turkey story on page 15, where I cooked both a turkey and a ham for the family Thanksgiving celebration!

MARK'S DUTCH OVEN HONEY MUSTARD HAM

Tools

12-inch deep dutch oven
12 coals below
14 coals above

Ingredients

1 medium-sized bone-in ham
1/2 cup honey
1/2 cup deli mustard
1/2 cup soy sauce
8–10 whole cloves

I started by putting the ham in the dutch oven. I actually had to cut it up into a few big chunks to make it fit and saved one chunk in the fridge for later. This would have been better in my 14-inch oven, but that was being used by the turkey. I also sliced diagonals back and forth across the surface of the ham to let the seasonings seep in.

I mixed all the other ingredients in a bowl and then smoothed them over the surface of the ham.

Then I put it on the coals. The ham had a lot of liquid, so as I baked it, from time to time I'd open up the dutch oven, scoop up the liquid, and baste it over the meat. I cooked the ham for three hours, just as long as the turkey.

Keeping the heat on was tricky. I went through a lot of coals. You have to watch the under coals, because it's easy to pay attention to when the coals on top are burning down, but the ones on the bottom need to be replaced too.

It was a great family party, and it was wonderful to have a choice between the two meats or to have both!

SLOW ELK ROAST

One day, a friend of mine was in a quandary. His son had left their garage freezer door open, and much of the meat stored in it had thawed. He messaged me on Facebook and asked if I wanted some elk roasts. While I felt sorry for his loss, it was about to be my gain!

I picked it up and did some web searching to find some good recipe ideas. Fortunately, there were plenty! Elk tastes a lot like beef, but can often have a tangy, gamey taste with some bitter tones as well. The final taste depends a lot on how it was processed in the field. Surprisingly, using an acid in the cooking, like a vinegar or a fruit juice, can tame the wild taste.

Tools

12-inch deep dutch oven
20+ coals below
10–12 coals below
12–14 coals above

Ingredients

4–6 lbs. elk roast (boneless)
4–6 cloves of fresh garlic, halved
olive oil to brown the roast
salt
pepper
herbs (sage, rosemary, parsley)

1 cup cranberry juice
2 cups beef stock

1 large onion, quartered
3–6 stalks celery
3–4 carrots
4–6 roma tomatoes
3–4 potatoes, in larger cubes, or a
    dozen small baby potatoes

I started by using a paring knife to cut some deep gashes in the meat, on both sides, and I stuffed the halved garlic cloves in the holes. Then, I salted and peppered each side and rubbed on the dried herbs. I set that aside so the meat could absorb the flavors.

While that was happening, I set some coals on to burn, and when they were white, I put them under the dutch oven, with a little olive oil in the bottom.

When the dutch oven and the oil were heated, I put in the elk roast pieces (there were two) and let them sear on each side. Then, I reset the coals to have some on top and some underneath, as the numbers up above represent. I added some fresh coals into the chimney also to begin heating. I added in the cranberry juice and the beef stock. My intent was to keep the internal temperature of the dutch oven between 250 and 300 degrees and to roast and braise it for a long time. That would tender it up, and the harsh acidity of the cranberry juice would lessen any of the gamey flavor.

After about an hour, I chopped up and added the vegetables. Cooking this meal was relaxing. I just kept refreshing the coals. I cooked it for over three hours. In between all that, I even made an apple pie!

Every once in a while, I would take a couple of forks and pry at the meat. When it came apart easily, it was done, and I brought it in. I let it rest with the lid on for a while (with no coals, of course). While it was resting, I used a basting syringe to pull out the juices, and I got that boiling in my 8-inch dutch oven. I whisked together about 2 tablespoons of flour and 1/4 cup water in a bowl and gradually stirred that into the boiling juices to make a gravy.

It was delicious! The meat was nice and not gamey at all.

VENISON MEATLOAF WITH TOMATO-APPLE SAUCE

For a picture of this recipe, scan this QR code:

When I was up at the campground with all of our friends who have children with special health care needs, I got to meet a few new friends. Saturday morning, a few of us dutch oven guys brought our pots together and we made mountain man breakfast for everyone.

Another father there, also named Mark, was enthusiastic about dutch ovening, and he and I got to talking about game meats. He's an avid hunter, and I have relatively little experience cooking wild game. I got a lot of good ideas and tips from him, and we had a lot of fun talking together.

So, when I came back, I remembered that I had a few pounds of ground game. It had been given to us by my sister-in-law. It was wrapped but unlabeled in our freezer. I suspect it was elk, but I'm not certain. I wracked my brain trying to think of something to do with it, and after some research, I settled on a few meatloaf recipes to blend together.

If an animal has been field-dressed well, it will go a long way toward removing the gaminess of the flavor. Acids and herbs can do much for that as well. There are plenty of both in this recipe, in the meat and in the sauce.

Tools

12-inch dutch oven
10–12 coals below

18–24 coals above
8-inch dutch oven
10–12 coals below

Meatloaf
Ingredients

2 pounds ground venison
2 large eggs
2 (8 oz.) cans tomato sauce
1 medium onion, finely chopped
1 1/2 tsp. sea salt
1/2 tsp. freshly ground black pepper
2–3 Tbsp. mustard

2–3 Tbsp. apple cider vinegar
liberal sprinklings of
  parsley
  sage
  thyme
  oregano
not so liberal sprinklings of
  chili powder

2–3 large potatoes, quartered and
  sliced

Sauce
Ingredients

1/4 cup juices from the meat
3 small apples, peeled and grated
6 ounces tomato paste
1 small onion, diced
2 Tbsp. apple cider vinegar

2 tsp. paprika
2 tsp. cinnamon
1 tsp. salt
1/2 tsp. red pepper flakes
1/4 tsp. freshly ground black pepper

After thawing the meat in the fridge overnight, I started, as I usually do, by lighting some coals and letting them get a bit white.

The meatloaf was actually easy to make. I simply mixed everything up in a bowl (except the potatoes). Then I spread it around in the dutch oven. It was originally my intention to make a loaf mound of meat in the middle of the dutch oven and then scatter the potato bits around it to fill in. However, I think I actually had closer to three pounds of meat, so I was able to cover the whole dutch oven with some depth. So, I just tossed the potatoes evenly over the top.

It baked for probably about an hour before the internal temperature read 150 degrees. Really, it's fine if it goes over that.

About 15 minutes before it was done, I checked it, and it had a lot of liquid. I used a small ladle to spoon most of it off into the 8-inch dutch oven. Then I put the 8-inch on some coals. I had already peeled and grated the apples while I was cooking the meatloaf, so I added that to the 8-inch oven with all the other sauce ingredients and put the lid on. I let it simmer and boil a bit to blend the flavors and loosen the apple shreds a bit.

Finally, it was done. I let it cool and rest for about 15 minutes and served it with the sauce drizzled across the top. It was delicious!

VENISON STEW (ELK)

My brother-in-law, an avid hunter, gave us some elk steaks once. I wasn't sure how to cook them, but I was really excited to try. I did a lot of research and reading to find out how they're done, and two things stuck with me. One was that game meats are much leaner than typical beef, so they tend to dry out as you cook them. It's good then, to cook them with veggies and things that add moisture to them.

Another was that a bit of vinegar can help counteract the gamey taste. You can overdo it, it's true, but a touch will help mellow it out.

Tools

12-inch shallow dutch oven

Ingredients

2–3 medium onions, sliced
2–3 cloves of garlic, minced
1–2 lbs. red game meat (like I mentioned, I used elk)
1 can (about a cup and a half) beef broth
4–5 stalks celery, chopped
3 large potatoes, quartered and sliced
1 jalapeno, chopped
1 cup of carrots (baby or sliced)

lots of chopped, fresh parsley
about a quarter cup of vinegar (I used red wine vinegar)
salt
black pepper
3–5 Tbsp. flour

Other things you can add, if you wanna

chopped green onions
a can of diced tomatoes

Making this was pretty easy. In fact, the hardest part was getting the coals lit in the cold wind that day. Especially since I was out of lighter fluid.

Anyway, it got lit, and I scattered some coals below. I put some olive oil in the dutch oven and put it on the coals to heat up. I added the onions and the garlic to brown. Then I added the meat to brown. I added everything else except the flour. That was added and stirred in later.

From there, I cooked it with about 15 or so coals below and the same number above. I let it boil and simmer for about 2–3 hours. The potatoes and carrots were soft, and the flavors were all the way through the broth and the meat. I added the flour to thicken it up.

It was great!

VENISON CHILI

For a picture of this recipe, scan this QR code:

Over the years, I've discovered something interesting about chili. There's only about a million different recipes. Some are great, some are greater. Some are hot, others are hotter. Some have beans, some don't. Some have tomatoes, others don't. Some have meat, others don't. It's almost as if there's a challenge out there to see just how far away you can get and still call it chili.

Well, I thought, *how hard can it be? I mean, if there are so many different recipes, and you pretty much follow one of them, you can't really go wrong, then, can you?*

Then a friend of mine mentioned that the best way he'd ever had venison was in a chili, and that intrigued me. My brother-in-law is an avid hunter, and I thought I might get some venison from him.

Tools

12-inch dutch oven
10–12 coals below

Ingredients

1/3 cup red kidney beans, uncooked
1/3 cup pinto beans, uncooked
1/3 cup black beans, uncooked
1–2 lbs. venison stew meat
1 medium onion, chopped
1 yellow bell pepper, chopped
2 large tomatoes, chopped
2 Tbsp. chili powder

1 bay leaf, crumbled
1/2 tsp. paprika
1 Tbsp. salt
1 Tbsp. crushed red pepper
2 Tbsp. ground cumin
1 Tbsp. cumin seeds
1/2 Tbsp. ground cinnamon
black pepper to taste
about a cup of water

I spent a lot of time researching recipes and learning how to cook beans. I have this thing about starting from scratch, so I didn't want to use canned beans this time.

I started off with three different kinds of beans, which were red kidney, black, and pinto. The night before, I started soaking them. When I put them in the bowl with the water, it kinda looked like red, white, and blue. Cool! I'd read that adding baking soda to the soaking water makes them less gassy later on. I thought I'd try that, but I found this not to be the case. I thought about issuing a formal written apology to my coworkers the following day.

I changed the water in the morning and again when I got home from church. After church, I started the coals and put the beans in my 12-inch shallow oven. I'd heard that it could take a lot of time to cook beans, even after they'd soaked, so I was all ready to cook them for hours if necessary. I put the dutch oven over 15 or so coals and put on the lid, with no coals on top. In no time, it was boiling away. After a few minutes of boiling, I took some briquettes off to bring it to a simmer.

I lightly oiled my 8-inch dutch oven and set it on top of 8–9 coals. When that heated up, I put the venison stew meat in to brown. Before long, the meat was browned, and the beans were starting to soften. I put the meat in the beans and added about a cup of water.

Then, I started chopping the onions, pepper, and tomatoes. All of them went in. I blended all of the dry seasonings and added them as well. From that point on, it was just a matter of stirring and keeping the coals fresh so it could simmer. The total cooking time was about two hours.

When it was all done, I served it with shredded cheddar on top and some of my wife's homemade bread.

Also, when it's done, it's a good idea to get chili out of your oven as soon as possible, because the acid will eat away at the patina you've built up with all your seasonings.

DUTCH OVEN SALMON AND ASPARAGUS HOLLANDAISE

For a picture of this recipe, scan this QR code:

One day, as I was planning my month of dutch oven dishes, I had a clear idea in mind of what I was going to cook the last Sunday of that month. Very clear, that is, until my wife spoke up.

"I want salmon!" She said with a finality that unlaid my best-laid plans. "Salmon with asparagus and a hollandaise sauce! With poofy rolls."

Well, I was more mouse than man. It was an easy choice, really, since I was intrigued with the idea, especially with the sauce. I'd never done a hollandaise. I wasn't even certain if I'd tasted one. I wondered about that out loud.

"It shouldn't be too difficult."

"Yeah? How do you do it?"

"Just buy one of those little packets."

"Oh, no. No. This is my chance to learn something new and test myself. I'm not going to just buy a little packet."

It worked out well. I did learn a lot about the sauce. One important thing I learned was that it's crazy to do a hollandaise sauce outdoors in a dutch oven in the middle of winter.

But, as I said, it all turned out well.

Salmon and Asparagus

Tools

12-inch shallow dutch oven
22+ coals below
10–12 coals above, later in the recipe

Ingredients

1 large filet of fresh salmon, cut into 2- to 3-inch wide chunks
juice of 4–5 limes
1/2 cup fresh cilantro
1/2 cup fresh parsley
salt
pepper
paprika
chili powder

3–4 fresh asparagus spears per guest
olive oil
kosher salt

Rice

Tools

10-inch dutch oven
14–16 coals below, maybe more

Ingredients

1 1/2 cups rice
3 cups water or stock
1/2 cup fresh cilantro
1/2 cup fresh parsley
2 (2 oz.) pkgs. sliced almonds
juice of two limes

Hollandaise Sauce

Tools

8-inch dutch oven
12+ coals below
glass or metal bowl, slightly larger than the dutch oven

Ingredients

water

4 egg yolks
1 Tbsp. freshly squeezed lemon juice
1/2 cup unsalted butter, melted (1 stick)
pinch cayenne
pinch salt

I cut the salmon into chunks and put them into a zip-top bag, along with all the flavorings in the first set of the list. I shook the bag to coat the salmon evenly and let it sit in the fridge for an hour or so while I made biscuits. I used an ordinary biscuit recipe and added shredded cheddar and minced garlic to the dough. (The Dutch Oven Drop Biscuit recipe is on page 11.)

I prepared the rice next. I put all of the rice ingredients into the 10-inch dutch oven and put it on the proper number of coals. I watched it while I cooked the salmon and other things and noted when it boiled. About 10–15 minutes after, I pulled it off the coals, without opening the lid, and let it steep and steam while the other parts of the dish finished.

The salmon was the third part to go on. I put a little olive oil in the bottom of my 12-inch shallow dutch oven and set it on the coals. I wanted it to get really hot. When I laid the salmon pieces in it, the sizzling and the immediate aroma let me know how good it was going to taste!

After a few minutes, when the down side of the fish had a little browning going on, I turned the pieces over with some tongs and closed the lid. I had a lot of salmon in the pot, so it wasn't cooking fast, even though it was initially hot. With the lid on, I put some coals on top to let it bake.

I shook the asparagus and its seasonings in a baggy and laid them across the top of the salmon pieces and replaced the lid.

Finally, I turned my attention to the hollandaise.

Before I began working with the ingredients, I put about a cup of water in the dutch oven and put it on the coals with the lid on. I started by separating the eggs and putting the yolks in a glass bowl I had prefitted to my 8-inch dutch oven. I juiced in the lemon and began whisking. I had to whisk for quite a while. It blends, but for a long time it doesn't change much. Then suddenly, it changes from a runny, almost orange liquid to a light yellow, thick, creamy texture.

By then, the water was boiling outside. Here's where there was a lot of compromise going on. On the one hand, a vigorous rolling boil is too hot. On the other hand, it was freezing cold outside, and I had to overcome that. I took off the lid and set the glass bowl over the dutch oven. I had chosen the bowl to cover the dutch oven like a lid but to not have the bottom resting in the boiling (or simmering) water. I knew the bowl wouldn't seal completely, so the boiling water would cool quickly.

With the bowl on the dutch oven over the simmering water, I continued whisking the egg mixture in the glass bowl. The idea is to temper the egg, or, that is, to raise the temperature slowly so it cooks but it doesn't scramble. I poured the melted butter into the egg mixture gradually while still whisking. I had no idea what I was doing, but eventually it did heat up, and it went from a smooth, creamy texture to a slightly thicker, creamier texture. Along the way I added in the pinch of salt, paprika, and cayenne.

By the time I was done with that, the salmon and asparagus were done, and the rice was ready for us as well. I spooned out a serving of the rice and laid the salmon pieces on top of it. The asparagus went to the side but was also still on the rice. Then, across it all, I drizzled the sauce. Finally, the biscuit made the meal complete.

Did it work? My wife said it was better than any restaurant. I love it when she says that!

DUTCH OVEN SHRIMP BISQUE

For a picture of this recipe, scan this QR code:

Once we went to a really fancy Italian restaurant, and my sons both tried the lobster bisque. They had heard some comedian talking about it, so they had to try it. Well, of course, they loved it.

I tasted it, too, and I was really impressed. Naturally, when I'm impressed, I want to try to make it. So, I did some research and found some good recipes. Unfortunately, lobster is expensive. I decided to do it with shrimp, which, of course, isn't cheap either, but at least it's not as pricey as lobster.

It has a lot of steps, but it's very flavorful because of the shrimp stock you make!

Tools

Two 12-inch dutch ovens,
each with 20+ coals below

Ingredients

2–3 lbs. shrimp
6–8 cups water
1 (14 oz.) can tomato paste

1 1/2 medium onions
3–4 stalks celery, including leaves
3–4 carrots

fresh parsley
salt
pepper
chili powder
lemon juice

6 cups heavy cream
1/4 cup cornstarch

You can approach this bisque in several ways. One way is to use uncooked, unshelled shrimp. Another is to use shrimp that are uncooked, deveined (but still in the shell). A third is to use whole shrimp, complete with the heads. The more complete the shrimp is, the more flavor you'll have in your stock. It's more work, but I recommend the whole shrimp. It doesn't really make a lot of difference how big the shrimp is either. For this instance, I used uncooked, unshelled shrimp (no heads) that are about the size you normally see in shrimp platters.

I started out with one of my 12-inch shallow dutch ovens, covered, with water. Once the water was boiling, I tossed in the shrimp and watched them turn that sweet pink-orange shade and curl. If you cook the shrimp too long, they get rubbery.

Once the shrimp were done, I pulled them out of the water but left the dutch oven on the coals.

I doused the shrimp in cold water while I peeled the shells and tails and deveined them. I threw away the veins, of course, but the shells and tails (and heads if you've got them) all went back into the stock to boil some more. I set aside the shrimp meat, reserving it for later. Once all the shrimp shells and parts were happily boiling away, I added the tomato paste.

I put the lid on and let it boil for a long time. How long? Well, that kinda depends on how much time you have. The longer it boils, the more flavorful the stock. I let it go for about an hour.

Near the end, I put a second dutch oven on some coals, with just a bit of oil in the bottom, and I started dicing the veggies. I tossed them in the second dutch oven and cooked them until they were soft. Then, I took them off the coals and mashed them with the back of a slotted spoon. It's a coarse mash, and that's okay.

I strained all the garbage out of the stock and added the smashed veggies. Then I added all of the seasonings. Finally, I added the cream and let it heat and simmer for another half hour. As it was simmering, I made a slurry of the cornstarch and water, enough to make it loose and runny (no clumps). I added the slurry about a tablespoon at a time to thicken the bisque. A hint: allow time between each dose of starch for it to affect the soup; otherwise, you'll add too much.

Finally, just before serving, I stirred the shrimp meat back into the soup to warm it up to serving temperature. Once it was ready, I ladled it into the bowls. It was delicious! I think it would also be great to serve in a bread bowl.

CHAPTER 5

SPECIALTY MAIN DISHES

A LOT OF DISHES AROUND THE WORLD make you scratch your head and say, "What?" A follow-up question might also be, "Can that be done in a dutch oven?"

I've spent a lot of time over the years at marksblackpot.com, searching for dishes that aren't supposed to be done in the black pots. I've tried things that are off the beaten path. This chapter is all about those, as well as a nice place to include some more traditional main dishes that don't fit well into other categories.

Some of these are personal creations, and some are inspired by other recipes and dishes I've seen. One of them was sent in by a guest blogger. Regardless of the source, I hope you'll give these a try. They're delicious and amazing to look at, even if the first look is a bit skeptical.

CHICKEN ARTICHOKE SOUP

For a picture of this recipe, scan this QR code:

There are a few ingredients that you can use in a dish that will immediately class it up. It almost doesn't matter how you use them. Just the fact that they are in there (and in the title) will immediately make foodies like me sit up and take notice. Without it, the dish is pleasant, but with it, the plate becomes a gourmet delight! A well-seasoned and grilled chicken breast is nice, for example, but if you put steamed asparagus next to it on the plate, it gets an extra star in the rating right away!

Artichoke is another one of these.

About two weeks ago, I had this germ of an idea for a dish with a chicken soup and a fresh half artichoke. I looked at various artichoke soups online, and most of them involved canned or bottled pickled artichoke hearts, veggies, and broth, simmered and then pureed. So, what you got was a thicker, creamier sort of soup.

That sounds great, but it wasn't what I was imagining. In fact, I couldn't find anyone who had done what I had in mind. This was encouraging, but it also made me nervous.

Tools

12-inch dutch oven
20–24 coals below

Ingredients

1 Tbsp. oil
1 can mushrooms or 1 cup fresh mushrooms, sliced
3 cups cooked chicken, shredded or cubed
2 medium onions, sliced
3 stalks celery, chopped
2 sweet peppers, diced

4–5 cloves garlic, minced
salt

2 Tbsp. oil
4 Tbsp. flour

1 cup milk
4 cups chicken stock
juice and zest of 2 lemons
parsley
oregano
salt
pepper

3 artichokes

This soup is created in steps, or layers. First, I browned and sautéd the veggies to get the maximum amount of flavors. I did this in a specific order so that those having to cook longer were started first. Then, I made a roux to help thicken the mix and created the soup. Finally, I added the artichoke halves to cook while the soup simmered.

To get started, I put the 12-inch dutch oven on some hot coals, with a little drizzle of oil in the bottom. I let that heat up for about 10–15 minutes. While that was happening I prepared the chicken and the veggies.

A word about the chicken. I had some pulled chicken from when I had previously made some stock. After eating a roast chicken or turkey, I boil the remainder (the bones and the rest of the meat), and the liquid becomes stock for soups. (See the following page.) I also pull the remaining meat off the bones and shred it for things like this, enchiladas, and sandwiches. For this meal, you can also use canned chicken chunks (well drained and dried), or even cubed, fresh chicken. If you use fresh chicken, you'll need to cook it a bit longer in the first step.

When the dutch oven was hot, I tossed in the chicken and let it sear. I added the mushrooms and let them cook down. I really like the mushrooms when they're nicely browned. Finally, I added in the other veggies. All the while I tossed and stirred everything frequently.

Once the veggies were getting a bit soft and the onions were translucent, I pushed everything aside and made a space in the middle of the dutch oven. In this space I added more oil and the flour. I immediately stirred it into a roux and let it cook. I stirred it until it started smelling a bit nutty. It was still light, a blonde roux. I mixed everything together.

Then, I stirred in the milk, the stock, and the flavorings. As always, you can use whatever flavors and amounts you like. I put the lid on, refreshed the coals, and brought it to a simmer for about 15 minutes. I tasted and adjusted it. Artichoke has some bitter tones, so the acid in the lemon juice goes a long way toward lessening that and livening it up. Make sure you have enough. Vinegar can also be used.

While it was simmering, I prepared the artichokes. I cut them in half across the stem so that each half was like a floral bowl. I trimmed off a few of the lower leaves. I got a paring knife and cut and scraped out the choke, which is the fuzzy stuff in the heart. I also cut out the first couple of layers of innermost leaves just to make sure I got everything. Then, I put those into the soup. I pushed them down into the mix and ladled soup over them so that the soup would get in between the leaves. I set the timer for 45 minutes and put the lid back on. During the 45 minutes, I adjusted the coals and occasionally checked and stirred it.

When it was finally done (a leaf of the artichoke came off freely), I brought it in to cool. I served it by lifting an artichoke half into a bowl and ladling the soup around it. I served it with some pita wedges to dip into the soup. We ate it by pulling off the leaves and scraping the flesh at the bottom of the leaf with our teeth and sipping the soup with a spoon. It was delicious!

CAULIFLOWER SOUP

This one was all my wife's idea. I like cauliflower okay, but I'm not a big fan of it. She found a recipe that looked interesting, so I thought I'd give it a go. Interestingly enough, if I'd used a veggie stock for the base instead of chicken broth (and without the ham), it could have been a vegetarian dish (depending, of course, on the kind of vegetarian you happen to be).

Like we sometimes do, we disagreed on one important point. She wanted me to make the recipe just as it was. I guess she wanted to see how close it was to the restaurant dish it was supposed to be mimicking. So, after I made it tame and straight for her, I pulled about a third of it off and mixed in my own flavorings (including the ham). So, since I'm writing the blog, this recipe is mine, and if you want, you can flavor yours however you like.

Tools

12-inch dutch oven
20–24 coals below

Ingredients

8 Tbsp. (1 stick) butter
2 medium onions
4–5 cloves minced garlic
salt

pepper
1/2 cup flour

2 cups half-and-half
2 cups milk
1–2 tsp. nutmeg
2 (14.5 oz.) cans chicken broth
2 1/2 lbs. chopped cauliflower

(Ingredients cont. on following page)

(Ingredients cont. from previous page)

1 Tbsp. mustard
juice of 1 lemon (with zest, if you like)
1 tsp. red pepper flakes
parsley

2–3 cups cheddar
2 cups cubed ham
1/4 to 1/2 cup grated Parmesan
1/4 cup fresh, chopped chives

I started by lighting the coals, and, when they were white, I counted them out and put my dutch oven over them to heat up. While that was being prepared, I minced the garlic and diced the onions. I melted the butter and put in the onions and the garlic. I also added the salt and pepper. When the onions were translucent and the garlic was brown, I added the flour and stirred it all up. I let it cook for a while, stirring constantly, until I could smell the rich nuttiness along with the garlic.

Then, I mixed in all the liquids. I stirred them up and put the lid on. I had to keep replenishing the coals underneath. It's important to be careful, because if you get too much goin' on under there, you can burn the liquid onto the bottom of the pot. I also stirred it a lot. Once it got bubbly, I was even more careful with the heat to maintain a simmer instead of a rolling boil. The main idea in this step is to cook the cauliflower. It takes about 15 minutes once the bubbles come.

When the cauliflower is cooked, it's time to chop and blend it all up. I could have used our hand blender, but I knew I'd need more oomph, so I used our electric immersion blender. I had to angle it so that the chunks of cauliflower could get under the blades. Blend it to your desired consistency.

After it's blended, start adding in the flavors you'd like. I included the ones I have here because they were easy to grab, and I think they made a really good combination of sour and sweet, along with the richness of the cream. I let them simmer for a while, stirring frequently.

In the last few minutes of cooking, I added the ham and cheeses. The cheeses melt into the soup and bond with the flour, milk, and cream. Without the flour, it would be a chunky, melted mess.

Finally, it was done. I served it with the chopped chives as a garnish on top.

SPLIT-PEA SOUP IN A BREAD BOWL

To get the book, scan this QR code:

I love making split-pea soup. It has to be the ultimate comfort food. For me, as a dutch oven cook, it's especially cool, because I usually do it within the week after I've cooked a big, delicious bone-in ham. The bone usually has a lot of meat still attached to it, and the meat and the bone is steeped in the spices and flavorings that I used on the ham. So each time I make the soup, it's completely unique.

This time Brendon had the brilliant idea of putting the soup in the bread boules I was making that morning. You can use about any bread flavor, but this time, the italian bread was perfect. (See page 140 for the italian bread recipe. For your convenience, this split-pea soup recipe is also found on page 141.) It's a little sweet from the sugar, but not much. Most of the flavor is from the flour itself added to the savory tang of the ham and the split-pea soup. Amazing!

The end result is a delicious, rich, and even elegant meal.

One weekend I was doing a lot of yard work. Even though I was working in the garden, I still wanted to cook. I wanted something simple and easy—a two-step, one-pot meal. I found an old ham bone from one of my past dutch oven roasting days buried in the freezer. Time for split-pea soup!

I had made split-pea soup many times before, but this time I kicked it up a notch. It must've worked, because even though I cooked up an entire 12-inch dutch oven of the stuff, there were no leftovers. That's good too, because split-pea soup doesn't usually make great leftovers. It ends up less of a soup and more of a paste.

I've found, by the way, that when you do these recipes, your final result will vary a little based on the way you cooked your ham. Some of the residual flavors and spices from the ham will carry over into the soup. I like that. It gives a little variety. The same is true if you make your own chicken stock.

Tools

12-inch dutch oven
15–20 coals below

Ingredients

1 sliced onion
4–5 cloves of garlic, minced
2 stalks chopped celery
6 cups water, at least half of which can be chicken stock
1 lb. bag of dried split peas
1 ham bone with lots of meat left on it.
1 diced potato
generous shakes of oregano, parsley, and chili powder
salt and coarse ground pepper to taste

I started by lighting up the coals and letting them start to get white. I put about a tablespoon of olive oil in the bottom of my dutch oven and let that heat up. Meanwhile, I chopped up the veggies.

Once the oil was hot, I dropped in the onion, garlic, and celery to sauté. Remember, if it's hot enough, they'll sizzle as soon as you drop them in. I stirred them and salted them a little. The dutch oven was plenty hot, and pretty soon they were browning.

Once the garlic was brown and the onions were translucent, I poured in the liquid. Then I added all the other ingredients, except the herbs and chili powder, and brought the soup back up to a boil.

Once it was simmering, I added in the herbs and chili powder. I added the chili powder a bit at a time. I'd shake in some, let it simmer for 15 minutes or so, and then taste it. I'd add more, wait, and taste it. I wanted it to have an edge, but I didn't want it having a recognizable chili taste. In the end, I probably added a little under a teaspoonful. Season with salt and pepper to taste, but be cautious, because the ham will add lots of salty flavor already.

It turned out great! We all gathered around our new patio table and had a wonderful outdoor meal. Again, we hollowed out the italian bread boules and did the "soup in a bread bowl" thing. If you try this one, let me know how it goes!

CHICKEN NOODLE SOUP WITH HANDMADE NOODLES

As I was planning my Sunday meal one weekend, a number of factors played into what I ended up making. First, my father-in-law was coming, so I wanted it to be something yummy. Second, it was getting colder, so it would need to be something warm and comforting. I was also thinking about my (then) upcoming book *Around the World in a Dutch Oven*. I thought about the handmade pasta recipes and how hard it is to describe the process. I thought it would be cool to make a video of the mixing and rolling. Then chicken noodle soup came to mind. That would be a perfect dish to satisfy all three requirements! I hadn't made noodles by hand in a long time, so I thought it would be fun to do that again.

Noodles
Ingredients

2 cups flour
2 tsp. garlic powder
1–2 Tbsp. parsley, basil, or oregano (or a combination)
6 eggs

Making the pasta is easy but a bit tricky to master. I recommend watching my video by scanning the QR code on the following page. In this video, I'll show you how to do it. If you can't access the video, I've also explained the process.

The first thing I did was to mix everything up. I made a mountain on the countertop with the flour and dug a well or hole in the middle of it. It looked like a volcano of flour and dry ingredients. Then I put the eggs in the middle and mixed them into the dry ingredients with a fork. It got all over. Still, I managed to not get it on the floor, but the area I was scooping kept getting bigger and bigger.

Once it was all mixed, I kneaded it for about 4–8 minutes, just like I knead bread, shaking bits of flour on the table as I go. I want it to be pliant and have some of gluten's stretchiness, but it won't be like a bread dough. Then I set it on the table to rest for a while. It's also good to chill it.

Then, I got my stick! About a week before, when I was preparing for this event, I bought a yard-long, 1 1/2-inch dowel. A simple rolling pin wasn't gonna cut it. It simply would not be wide enough. Still, I could tell that three feet was gonna be too much for my little kitchen counter, so I cut about a foot off one end. I also rubbed veggie oil into the wood to help it not stick to the dough.

I started by rolling the dough into a disc that was a little under a foot in diameter, just like I would do with a normal rolling pin. Then I rubbed on a light layer of flour, flipped the far edge up and over, and rolled it up. Then I started the rolling and stretching process.

Here's how it works: I applied a bit of rolling pressure as I moved the stick toward me. I released the pressure and slid the stick (without rolling it) away from me. Then I rolled it toward me again. Actually, I was doing a back and forth rocking motion as I rolled the stick toward me. While I was doing this, I was moving my hands outward to help stretch the dough side to side.

I unrolled it from the stick, turned it a little on the countertop, rolled it up again, and worked it the same way—just like in the video. Each time I unrolled it, I watched to see if it was sticking. If so, I smoothed on some flour. Gradually, it got thinner and thinner, and bigger and bigger. I gotta tell you just how gooooooood it smelled while I was rolling it out. Those herbs and the garlic had me in heaven.

Finally, I folded it up and sliced it. Really, I probably sliced it too thick to call it true fettuccine. Sue me. After slicing it, I lightly tossed it with my fingers to separate it and left it on the tabletop to dry a little. I didn't let it dry out though. I could have, but I didn't. Then it wouldn't have been pasta fresca but rather pasta secca (fresh pasta or dried pasta).

For a video of this process, scan this QR code:

Soup

Tools

12-inch dutch oven
20+ coals below

Ingredients

3–4 boneless, skinless chicken breasts
4–6 cups water (to fill the dutch oven about halfway)

noodles (that you just made)
3–4 carrots
1–2 medium onions
3–4 stalks celery
1–2 sweet peppers
salt
pepper
juice of 1 lemon

I started by lighting up some coals and getting them under the dutch oven (with the lid on) with the chicken and the water. I let it boil until the chicken was essentially cooked all the way through. I wasn't too concerned, because it would cook more in the soup. While that was happening, I was chopping up the veggies.

Once it was done, I pulled the chicken breasts out and refreshed the coals underneath. I put the lid back on and let the broth come to a good, energetic boil. I added in the pasta and replaced the lid. After a few minutes, I stirred it gently. I didn't want it to cook too much or too quickly.

Then, I added in all the veggies. I cut the meat into chunks and added that back in. I added in the flavorings and seasonings and let it simmer with the lid on until the veggies were soft.

It was a delicious soup! A big hit with my family and my father-in-law. Because there were big chunks of veggies and meat and a lot of noodles, it was a hearty and filling dish. The residual flour on the noodles and the starch of the noodles also helped thicken the broth.

FRIENDSHIP FISH SOUP

I have some good friends across the street. They're a young couple. He's a techie and a graphic designer. One summer, he went fishing and gave me some of the fish he'd caught. He also made me some fish soup. Man, it was delicious! It was a mess to eat though, because the fish was cut up into chunks. It was gutted and scaled but not filleted. You eat the broth and veggies with a spoon, and you pull the fish meat off the bones with your fingers—it's a mess. If you eat this stuff, you'll want to be with good friends.

Since it's his recipe and method and he gave me the fish, and because I invited him and his wife over to sample it, I'm calling it "Friendship Fish Soup."

Tools

12-inch dutch oven
20–24 coals below

Ingredients

4–6 cups water
2–3 medium fish
4–5 medium onions, sliced
4–5 stalks celery, sliced
5–6 cloves garlic, sliced
1 small-medium zucchini, quartered
   and sliced
4–5 medium carrots, sliced

1–2 green peppers, sliced
1 jalapeno, cored, seeded, and
   sliced
bay leaves
basil
1/4 cup lemon juice, to taste
1 Tbsp. salt, to taste
pepper to taste

This is an easy dutch oven recipe to make. You slice up the veggies, cut up the fish, and put them in the dutch oven. Then you place the oven on the coals and cook the soup.

I gutted, scaled, and cleaned the fish. Since it was summer, I froze them. Then, on the day I cooked them, I got them out of the freezer in the early afternoon and let them thaw. If you're fortunate to have freshly caught fish, you wouldn't have to thaw them, but they'd still need to be gutted and scaled. I sliced off the tails and fins and cut the fish into four, two–inch chunks. I put the chunks into the dutch oven—bones, skin, and all. I added all the other ingredients and put the oven on the coals and covered it with the lid.

Really, you can do this with whatever veggies you have on hand. I went really heavy on the onions, because I like a soup that has some good veggie substance to it. Potatoes would have been another good one to add. Noodles or rice would have also worked. I like keeping the broth clear though, because you're gonna be sticking your fingers in it. . . .

Every 15 minutes or so, check it and taste the broth. Add salt, pepper, and the seasonings you like. You can add a bit more jalapeno, or only core half the jalapeno you add so that there's a bit more heat, if you like it that way.

I really liked it. My wife wasn't as enthused by it and didn't like the idea of picking fish bones out of her soup, so she only had the veggies. Still, we had a great time visiting with our friends, and I really like the recipe. Every once in a while, I make something that I like, even though hardly anyone else likes it.

CHILE VERDE FOR CINCO DE MAYO

From My Blog

"So, today is Cinco de Mayo. This is really more of an American holiday than a Mexican one. It's not even a national mandatory holiday. Originally, it celebrates a victory over the French at the battle of Puebla in the 1860s. Now, it's a chance for Mexicans in America to celebrate their heritage. So, for a day we all get to be Mexican, kinda like on St Patrick's Day when we all get to be Irish.

"At any rate, on this holiday, I made some Chile Verde. As usual, I gathered this recipe from a number of sources, mostly from the good folks at the Dutch Oven Cooking Yahoo Group.

"Here's the recipe I used. I don't know how authentic it is, but man it was tasty!

Tools

12-inch dutch oven
lots of coals below

Ingredients

1 yellow onion, chopped
2 Tbsp. minced garlic
2 Tbsp. olive oil
3 lbs. lean pork, cubed

3 mild anaheim chilies, seeded and
   sliced
1 jalapeno, sliced (or more to taste)
   (In retrospect, this verde turned out
   pretty mild. I'd have added another
   jalapeno or two.)

8 large tomatillo, husk peeled and
   coarsely chopped
2 tsp. oregano
2 tsp. ground sage
1 1/2 tsp. ground cumin
1/4 cup chopped fresh cilantro
1 tsp. dried ancho chile powder
2 Tbsp. lemon juice
1 cup chicken stock
1/2 tsp. salt (to taste)
1/4 tsp. white pepper
2 tsp. cornstarch

"First, I got some coals going, and I sliced up the onions. I put the oil in the bottom of the dutch oven and added the onions, garlic, and pork. I put it all on the coals to brown.

"Then, in a bowl, I chopped up all the other veggies (I'd never used tomatillos for anything before) and added the spices. The amounts here were from a composite recipe. They're good guidelines, but I didn't stick too close to them.

"Once the meat was browning, I added everything else and let it boil with the lid on for about 45 minutes. Then, to let it boil down some more, I let it simmer uncovered for another 45 minutes to an hour. By that time the tomatillos had dissolved (like tomatoes do), and I added the cornstarch (mixed with a bit of water to help it dissolve) just for a titch of thickening.

"In the process of cooking, some neighbors were having friends over and invited us as well, so I took the whole pot over. He'd made some rice and heated up some black beans. I brought tortillas as well. They also had pork chops and veggies, and it made for a great pot luck party.

"When I eat Chile Verde, I like to mix in the rice and the beans, tear up a flour tortilla, and scoop up the mixture in the tortilla. I don't know if it's more or less authentic, but I like the taste of all the foods mixed in. The rice adds texture, the pork and the chile give great flavor, and the tortilla has a bit of a salty zing to it."

SHELF-SAFE SPAGHETTI

For a picture of this recipe, scan this QR code:

In the process of preparing the meals and recipes for my book on food storage, I've run into the problem of meats. The big question is, how to do meat dishes with shelf-stable ingredients.

Shelf-stable, of course, implies ingredients that can be pulled from long-term storage on a shelf. That does not include frozen meats. Don't get me wrong—it's a good thing to have a supply of frozen meats in your food storage. It's great to thaw out good meats and cook them. However, even they can be subject to freezer burn, and if your power goes out for more than a few days, you're in trouble.

This leaves three options: dried meat, canned meat, and fake meat. None of these are ideal, and we will all swear up and down that fresh meats are the best, because they are. However, if you use these properly, with good ingredients and seasonings, you can cook up dishes that are delicious and filling and still provide the protein you need.

I cooked up some things using shelf-stable meats one weekend in preparation for my book. One was the jerky chili, and another was a spaghetti sauce using beef-flavored TVP. (TVP is "Textured Vegetable Protein," a staple of the vegans.) TVP has a texture much like ground meat, carries various flavorings, and is made entirely from soy, so no animal products are in it. It is dried and stores forever. We had in our food storage a number of large cans of this stuff. The cans held various flavors, like chicken, beef, and bacon, but I was always afraid to try it. The mere thought of smooshy, fake meat made me run for the hills. But I tried it that weekend, and my results were good.

Tools

8-inch dutch oven
12+ coals below
10-inch dutch oven
16+ coals below

Ingredients

1 cup water, vegetable stock, or
   chicken stock
1 cup beef TVP
1 (14 oz.) can diced tomatoes
1 (6 oz.) can tomato sauce

2–4 Tbsp. dehydrated onions
2–4 Tbsp. dehydrated sweet peppers
1 (4 oz.) can mushrooms
salt
pepper
oregano
basil
crushed red pepper

3–4 cups water
salt
a handful of spaghetti noodles

I started by lighting some coals, and once they were hot, I set up the 8-inch dutch oven and the 10-inch dutch oven with their respective coals, with water in the 10-inch and stock in the 8-inch. I put the lids on and waited for them to boil.

The stock boiled first, so I dealt with it first. TVP should be mixed with boiling water at a 1:1 ratio, so I tossed in the cup of TVP and stirred it up. It absorbed the liquid almost instantaneously. I mixed in the tomatoes and the tomato sauce and stirred it up, replacing the lid. I pulled away some of the coals, because I wanted it to begin simmering and not to burn on the bottom.

Then, I added in all of the other flavorings and kept it simmering.

About then, the water in the 10-inch was boiling. I tossed in the spaghetti sticks and replaced the lid. In a few minutes, the noodles had softened, so I stirred them up to keep them from sticking.

After about 8–10 minutes, the spaghetti was *al dente*, which means it's not so soft. It still resists your teeth a little. I strained the spaghetti out of the water and served it on the plate smothered in sauce. I also sprinkled some Parmesan onto it, which, technically, isn't shelf-stable, but it's certainly more so than softer cheeses.

The final verdict? I was impressed. Had I not known it was TVP, I might have thought it was ground beef. In this particular dish, there are a lot of other flavors to distract the tongue, so not so much attention is paid to the flavor or the texture of the TVP. If I were to eat the TVP straight, or if it were a bigger part of the dish, I'm not sure how well it would do.

SPAGHETTI SQUASH WITH MEAT SAUCE

For a picture of this recipe, scan this QR code:

My mom made Spaghetti squash a lot when I was a kid, so I'm pretty familiar with it. For those who aren't, it's a yellow winter squash, and after it's cooked, the flesh is scraped off the rind. When you do it, the flesh shreds into short strings and looks a lot like spaghetti. It has a slightly sweet taste with a crunchy texture.

Lately, we've been trying to eat healthier, so we got a few squashes. I did some research and found that there are a lot of ways that people use them. Of course, there's the traditional italian tomato sauces that are served as a main dish, but there are also those that are served as a side, with butter, garlic, and herbs. Another cool thing is that it will keep on your countertop for weeks.

In this dish, I wasn't really going for healthy, because I used ordinary pork sausage. Still, I figured that a full plate was only about 700–750 calories, including the Parmesan and feta. That's not bad for a main evening meal. If you wanted to go even less, you could use ground turkey and spice it like a sausage.

Another comment: It was tricky to figure out how many spaghetti squashes to cook for how many people. For some reason, the websites I looked at didn't say either. I found that as a main dish, one squash will do a full plate for two people. As a side, one spaghetti squash could probably serve three to four.

Tools

14-inch deep dutch oven (to cook two
  squashes)
16–18 coals below
20–24 coals above

12-inch shallow dutch oven
18–20 coals below

Ingredients

2 spaghetti squashes
olive oil
salt

1–2 Tbsp. olive oil
2 medium onions
about 6 mushrooms

1 green pepper
4–5 garlic cloves, minced
salt

1 lb. ground meat (I used sausage)
1 (28 oz.) can diced tomatoes
1 (14 oz.) can tomato sauce
oregano
basil
salt
pepper

Parmesan cheese
feta cheese

I started out by lighting a lot of coals, because I'd be cooking both the squashes and the sauce side-by-side. Using a butcher knife, I cut the squash into two lengthwise pieces. It was tough, so I went with the big blade! I scooped out the seeds and the stringy guts and left the regular squash flesh in place. I drizzled some olive oil and salt in each half and put them into the oven upside down. I cut open the second one and did the same. If you place the pieces the other way, like a bowl, the moisture gets trapped as the squash cooks and makes the noodles runny.

The squash had to cook for a long time. If it hadn't, it would have cut down the time a bit. Once the squashes were in place, it was just a matter of maintaining the heat for about an hour and a half.

In the meantime, I made the sauce. It's a pretty straightforward spaghetti meat sauce, and if you wanted to, you could even use bottled sauce. But I made my own.

I started off with coals under my 12-inch dutch oven and heated up some olive oil. I sliced the mushrooms and sautéd them. My wife likes her mushrooms cooked down quite a bit, browned and done. Over the years, I've come to love them this way too. It takes a little longer though. Once they were close to being done, I added in the onions and peppers and finally the garlic. I added a bit of salt with each to help extract the moisture.

Once the veggies were a little brown, I cleared them off to the sides and put the meat in the center. I browned it fully and added the tomatoes (with liquid) and the sauce. Finally, I added the seasonings to taste and replenished the coals for a good simmer with the lid on.

When I could stick a little wooden skewer into the flesh of the squashes without much resistance, I knew they were done, and the sauce was well-simmered also. I brought it all in.

I let the squashes cool, with the lid off for a while, so they would be easier to handle. I pulled each one out, one at a time, and, with a fork, scraped the insides of the squash bowl lengthwise. Immediately it pulled apart into short threads, like pasta. I put it on the plate as I took it out of the oven. When the squash was empty, the plate was full, and I spread it out. I ladled on some of the sauce and sprinkled on the cheeses.

You eat it with a fork, but not like spaghetti, where you twirl it around. The noodles aren't long enough for that. You just scoop up a forkful and enjoy it! This was the first time my son remembered trying it, and he loved it!

CABBAGE AND SAUSAGE

I don't often use cabbage, but a couple of heads were given to us, and I had to think for a bit to figure out what to do with them. A slaw, of course, is an obvious idea, but that's uncooked. Finally, I picked up some smoked sausage and went with this!

This dish is a comfort food from my childhood. My mom used to make it in a slow cooker. I don't know the exact recipe she used, but I found a few that were close enough and blended them together.

Tools

12-inch dutch oven
20+ coals underneath, to brown and sauté
10–12 below, 16–18 above for the final cooking.

Ingredients

1–2 lbs. smoked sausage or kielbasa
1 Tbsp. butter
2 small onions, chopped

3 cloves garlic, minced
2 stalks celery, chopped
1/2 jalapeno, cored, seeded, and minced
1/8 tsp. ground black pepper
1 tsp. salt

1 small head cabbage, shredded
1 apple, cored and sliced thin
juice of 1 lemon
1 Tbsp. wine vinegar
1/2 cup water
salt

I started by getting the coals hot and then heating up the dutch oven over them. I wanted it pretty hot, so I let it sit for a bit. I sliced the sausage on the bias (or at an angle) so there'd be more surface area to brown and tossed them in. They started sizzling immediately, letting me know that the oven was hot enough. I tossed them around and let them get nice and seared.

I put in the butter and let it melt. While the sausage was sautéing, I chopped and minced the veggie ingredients, minus the cabbage. I tossed them in and stirred them to get them cooking. I let them sweat with the salt and pepper.

While that was cooking, in between stirrings, I prepped the cabbage. I took the dutch oven off the coals and put in the rest of the ingredients. I like it acidic, so I didn't scrimp on the lemon juice or the vinegar. I rearranged the coals and put the lid on, with coals on top. From there, it was a simple process to cook the cabbage down. I stirred it occasionally. It took about 25 minutes to a half hour, and I replenished my coals (partly due to time, and also because it was cold and breezy outside).

It's easy to serve. Just dish it out onto a plate or a bowl. In the end it was delicious! I liked the tangy tones of the lemons with the edgy sweet tones of the cabbage and the apple. The savory sausage is a nice touch too.

DANDELION DELICACIES

For a picture of these recipes, scan this QR code:

Late one summer, I read online where people actually cook and eat dandelions. I was repulsed but intrigued. I had heard of it in the past, but this time I saw some recipes and processes that caught my eye, and I determined to try it.

Unfortunately, at the time, It was kinda difficult to find the cute yellow flowers in bloom. Most in my neighborhood were well into seed at that point.

So, one day, as I was driving home, I happened to notice that the dandelion flowers were budding in force. It was also a bright, warm, sunny day (and we'd had precious few of those at the time), so I decided to jump on the opportunity and take a chance.

Of course, I had never cooked them before, nor had I eaten them. So, it was kind of a wild shot that it would even work, let alone taste good. I tried two different dishes—one with the greens, and one with the flower. They were not only edible but also palatable. It was an odd taste. It had tones of sweet and savory, depending on the dish, and also an underlying tone of bitter. But the bitter was really just an edge rather than the whole flavor. Like I said, it was odd. I don't think it's for everyone. In the end, I liked it.

I also need to explain that since this was the first time I'd tried it, there were things in the process that I might have done wrong. Well, not so much wrong, per se, but not in the best order. So, I'm writing this from the point of view of how I would do it next time.

Dandelion Greens

Tools

8-inch dutch oven
10–12 coals below

10-inch dutch oven
14–16 coals below

Ingredients

1 (12-inch) colander, filled to heaping with rinsed and trimmed dandelion greens.

2 cups water

2 Tbsp. salt

1 lb. bacon

1 medium onion

3 cloves garlic

salt

pepper

crushed red pepper

lemon or lime juice

The first step is to gather the dandelion plants. I went foraging in our neighborhood. I'll bet it was quite a sight—me, with my box of flowers and my hand shovel! I looked for plants that had lots of bushy leaves and plenty of large, round flowers. I looked in places that I thought hadn't been sprayed with herbicides. I didn't want to be eating toxic chemicals. I got a few from my own yard, but not many, because I had just mowed, so the leaves on most of my plants were chopped short. When I found a plant I wanted, I just dug around it until the root snapped and tossed the whole thing in my box.

It's good to get a whopping amount of dandelion plants for this project, because after you trim the leaves from the root structure and after those leaves cook down, there really isn't much there. So, start with lots, and you'll end up with plenty.

I prepared the greens first. After lighting up some coals on my porch, I worked indoors at my sink. I grabbed a dandelion plant and snapped off any usable flowers. Then I rinsed the remaining plant many times over. I separated the leaves from the longer flower stems and tore the leaves off just above where the green leaf starts to grow from the stem. I rinsed those leaves again and tossed them into the colander. I repeated this process for all of the plants I'd harvested.

At this point, the coals were ready, so I put them under the 8-inch dutch oven with the water and the salt. I also put more fresh coals in my side fire for the flower fritters.

While that was coming to a boil, I put coals underneath my 10-inch dutch oven and added the bacon to it, which I had cut into short, 1-inch bits. Then I diced and sliced the onion and minced the garlic.

Once the bacon was getting crispy, I used a spoon and pulled out most of the drippings. I tossed in the onion and the garlic to sauté.

By now, the water was boiling in the 8-inch oven, so I added the greens a few at a time. I let them boil, cooking them for 10–15 minutes.

While the greens were boiling and the onions and bacon were still sautéing, I made the flower fritters (see the following page). Once the greens were done and tender, I lifted them out with tongs and put them back into the colander over the dutch oven to drain a bit. Finally, I tossed them into the 10-inch dutch oven with the bacon and stirred it all up, sizzling it for a few minutes more. I added the seasonings at this point too, with particular emphasis on the lemon or lime juice. The juice goes a long way in tempering the bitter. I think that balsamic vinegar would taste great too.

At this point, things really don't need to cook any more. It's all done. You're just combining it and merging the flavors, so just serve it up. This really is a veggie side dish. In this case, since I was just trying it out, I served it on plate with the flower fritters.

My son was skeptical at first, but even he was impressed in the end.

FLOWER FRITTERS

It might be interesting to know that the name *dandelion* actually comes from an anglicization of the french *dent-de-lion*, meaning "lion's tooth."

Or not . . .

On the previous page, I talked about making the greens. Here, I'll instruct you on another fascinating dish: Dandelion Flower Fritters. I made them alongside the greens and served them together. They don't have to be done together, and, in a book, it's easier to break them into two separate recipes.

I'll refer you back to the previous page to learn how to harvest the dandelions.

Tools

10-inch dutch oven
14–16 coals below

Batter

Ingredients

4 Tbsp. veggie oil
1 cup milk
2 Tbsp. sugar
1 egg
1 cup flour, plus extra to get the right
  consistency

Other Ingredients

20–30 dandelion flower heads

pancake syrup or powdered sugar

I put the oil in the 10-inch dutch oven and placed it on the hot coals. While that was heating up, I mixed the batter. I put all of the batter ingredients into a bowl and whisked them up. I mixed it to be a little thicker than my typical pancake batter, which is usually pretty runny.

Once the batter was mixed and the dutch oven and oil were hot, I was ready. I picked up a flower by the green bud underneath, turned it over, and dunked it into the batter. Then I dropped it onto the bottom of the oven, where it sizzled nicely. There was a lot of room, so I did a lot of them. I just let them cook until the batter was done and then pulled them out, replacing them with more battered buds. It's pretty simple.

When it was all done, I plated them alongside the greens and drizzled them with pancake syrup. Another suggestion I'd read about was to sprinkle them with powdered sugar or dip them into ketchup or mustard.

The gentle sweetness of the batter and the syrup helped temper some of the bitter tang that came from the bud. The petals had a real lightness to them. It was a unique taste overall. If it's an acquired taste, I acquired it quickly!

STUFFED ARTICHOKE ON RICE

For a picture of this recipe, scan this QR code:

As I was surfing the 'net one day, looking for cool dutch oven sites, I revisited cooking-outdoors.com and found this great recipe for stuffed artichokes.

Instantly, my thoughts and memories went back to my childhood, when my mother steamed some artichoke heads and served them for dinner. We were used to strange and new things appearing on our plates, and most of it was good, so we tried them. Dad showed us how to pull out the leaves, dip them in the butter sauce, and scrape the tasty, pasty meat off the leaf with our teeth.

I still remember it as one of our many fun dinners. It was so different that it became not only a delicious meal that was good for us, but also an event that the family would remember for many years to come. At least, I would!

As soon as I saw this at www.cooking-outdoors.com, I knew I had to try it. And, of course, I couldn't just follow the original recipe. I have to try things a little differently! Some of the things I did that day were improvised at the moment. I'll try to recreate them as a recipe, with more exact measurements, but remember that the amounts are only guesses at best. When you cook them, I encourage you to improvise as well.

Tools

12-inch dutch oven
24+ coals below

8-inch dutch oven
12+ coals below

Ingredients

olive oil
1 medium onion, diced fine
3 celery stalks, diced fine
4–5 cloves garlic, minced
1/2 to 1 lb. mild italian sausage
salt
pepper
liberal shakes of dried parsley
dried oregano
dried basil

1 to 1 1/2 cups fine, dried bread crumbs

about 4 cups water
4 fresh artichoke heads

1/2 cup mayonnaise
1/4 cup commercially prepared salsa
salt
pepper
paprika
garlic powder
chili powder (add gradually, go light
    at first)
lemon juice

2 cups chicken broth
1 cup water
2 cups rice
remainder of the stuffing

The first thing I did was to get my 12-inch regular dutch oven heating on a lot of coals, with about a tablespoon or two of olive oil in it. It was a breezy March day, so I knew I was going to go through a lot of coals, and I would have to watch it close and manage the heat carefully.

Once the oil was shimmery, I dropped in the aromatic veggies (the onion, celery, and garlic). They simmered right away, and I cooked them until they started coloring brown a bit. Then I put in the sausage. When browning the sausage, I took great pains to work the meat so that it ended up cooking in very fine, small chunks. Big globs would be difficult to stuff into the artichoke leaves. At this point, I also added in the herbs and seasonings.

It will look like you're making too much filling to put in the artichokes. That's okay. Not only do they hold more that you think, but you'll also use the remainder later.

When the sausage was done, I pulled it out with a big serving spoon, working to get out as much as I could. Then I poured in the water. I refreshed the coals, and put the lid on, setting it to boil while I worked on the artichokes.

To finish the stuffing, I stirred in the bread crumbs. If you use preseasoned italian bread crumbs, by the way, I wouldn't worry about adding in all the herbs. I stirred it all up, and it mixed nicely. The crumbs absorbed the sausage grease very well. If it still looks too dry and unmanageable, you can add a bit of olive oil. I didn't. It clumped, but it was also a bit loose.

This was the first time I had done artichokes, so I had a great time learning how to prepare them for steaming.

- Using my kitchen shears, I snipped off a row of the bottom-most leaves and any leaf that was out on the stem.
- Then, going around the perimeter, I trimmed about 1/4 inch off the tip of every leaf in the head. Not only did it look nice, but it also made it much easier to stuff the artichoke.
- Once I got to the central part, I used my chef's knife to lop off the top half to 3/4 inch of the center. Then I used my thumb to pry it open and loosen and stretch the leaves.
- Finally, I cut off the stems.

Then, I stuffed the artichokes. I held them over a plate to catch all the leftover stuffing. I held it upright in front of me with one hand and used that hand's thumb to pry apart the leaves. I poured stuffing into the spaces with a spoon. I was surprised how much I could get into one head. Even still, there was about a third left over.

Back out to the dutch oven, where the water was boiling by now. I put each artichoke head into the dutch oven, stem down, side by side. All four fit pretty snugly. I put on the lid and marked the time. From that time on, it was only a matter of maintaining the coals on the bottom and checking at 20–30 minute intervals if the water was still there. I let these cook for about an hour and 15 minutes.

While they were cooking, I first made the sauce, and then the rice.

Like I said, the quantities of the ingredients of the sauce were pretty much improvised. I put in the mayo, then the salsa. I whisked those together and tasted them to make sure there was a balance. Then, I added the other ingredients and seasonings by shake. At each point, I tasted, until I felt there was a good balance. I did add the chili powder, but I didn't want this to be a hot dish. I just wanted some zing.

When there was only 20 minutes or so left in the cooking, I put on the rice, water, and stock. I noted when it started boiling by when it vented out from under the lid. From there I let it cook on the coals for about another 10 minutes. Then I took it off the coals and let it sit, covered, for another 10 minutes. Finally, I fluffed it with my fork and mixed in the remnant of the filling.

I served it up with a bed of rice with the flowery head of the artichoke on top. Off to the side was a small ramekin with the dipping sauce. I also made some small loaves of sourdough that day, so I included that in the picture.

If you've never eaten whole artichoke before, it really is a lot of fun. It's finger food. You grab one of the leaves by the tip and pull it off the head. It kinda acts like a spoon and catches the stuffing that was in that pocket. You dip the foot end into your sauce and put it in your mouth. You scrape the leaf against your upper teeth, scraping all of that soft stuffing and artichokey goodness off the leaf husk. Then you set the leaf on your plate and grab another.

It was a delicious meal. One of my sons fought us on the leaves, but he loved the rice. The other loved the entire thing. It was a family evening together that I'll treasure for a long time!

MARK'S DUTCH OVEN ACORN SQUASH BOATS

For a picture of this recipe, scan this QR code:

I saw some acorn squash in a store about a month ago, and I thought back to my childhood. I hated squash. I mean, I really hated it. Mom would boil it or steam it and then mash it up into this gooey pile on my plate.

Sorry, Mom. I didn't mean to throw you under the bus (figuratively, people). But c'mon! Wasn't there a better way?

So, standing there in the store, I imagined it the way I'd seen it in some cookbooks and magazines: halved and hollowed, with a savory meat filling. It inspired me to give it a try. I bought them and brought them home.

I spent a few days looking over cookbooks and 'net recipes. Many of them caught my eye, and I got many good ideas. The day I decided to make them, however, I did it on my own.

Tools

Two 12-inch dutch ovens
Oven 1: 16–18 coals above, 8–12 coals below
Oven 2: 18–22 coals below

Meat/Sausage
Ingredients

1–2 lbs. ground meat
1 Tbsp. garlic powder
1 Tbsp. kosher salt
1 Tbsp. paprika
1/2 Tbsp. black pepper
1/2 Tbsp. ground sage
1/2 Tbsp. ground oregano
1 tsp. crushed red peppers (less or
    more, to your liking)

Finishing Touches
Ingredients

fresh parsley
grated cheese

Squash Boats
Ingredients

2 acorn squash, halved and seeded
brown sugar
1 cup water

Filling
Ingredients

4–5 cloves garlic, minced
1 large red onion, diced
1 green sweet pepper, diced
3 stalks celery, sliced
kosher salt
1 medium tomato, diced
sausage you made previously
    (see above)

The first step was the meat. I wanted some sausage to give some edge to the dish, but we were out of it. It was on a Sunday, so I didn't want to go shopping. I looked for some ground meat, and I found some in our freezer, but I wasn't sure what it was. It looked like some game meat grind that a hunter friend of ours had given us. I think it was elk. Before church, I put it in some cool water to thaw.

After church, I got a bowl and started mixing in herbs and spices. I paid attention to what I put in and in what amounts so I could write it up later with some accuracy. That's what I have listed here. Adjust it to your taste and to the amount of meat you've got. Mine ended up a little too hot and spicy, so in the ingredients listed above, I've reduced the crushed red peppers—but only slightly. Since this was probably a game meat, I added some olive oil (it was obviously very lean) and a few dashes of vinegar to ease the gamey taste.

I set that aside in the fridge so that the flavors could seep in. It would still be a good hour or so before I would use it.

Then, I went out and lit up some coals.

While those were whitening up, I prepared the squash. I halved each one and scooped out the seeds and goop. I dusted (lightly) the inside of each one with a bit of brown sugar. I set them in one of my 12-inch dutch ovens, with a bit of water in the bottom, and set that on the coals, with more coals on the lid.

I put the other dutch oven on coals (just underneath it) to heat it up while I cut the veggies. I put everything in to sauté but the tomato. Once the onions were translucent, I added the tomatoes and stirred to cook. Finally, I pushed everything aside and added the meat in the middle. As it cooked, I mixed it all together.

While this was happening, I occasionally checked the flesh of the squashes for doneness. I'd stick them with a fork, and when it was soft and didn't resist, I knew they were done. I pulled them off the coals and removed them from the oven so I could pour out the water.

This was about the time that the filling mixture was done, so I put the squash boats back in the dutch oven and put a scoop or two of filling in each one. Even though I mounded it up pretty high, there was leftover, so that's good for a lunch. I sprinkled on the parsley and the cheese, and put it back on some fresh coals (over and under, with extra emphasis on over) to bake for a bit.

At this point, all of the food was cooked, so I didn't leave it on long. I just wanted to bake all of the flavors together and to melt and brown the cheese a bit. After that, I brought it in and served it up—a squash bowl in a ceramic bowl!

See, Mom? *My* kids *like* squash! :-)

SHEPHERD'S PIE

After several weeks of more strange and exotic recipes, I decided to do something more traditionally dutch oven. (Someone on the dutch oven cooking Yahoo group once said, "Mark'll try anything," which I took as a compliment!)

I was going through my new cookbooks and found a recipe for Shepherd's Pie. I looked it over and was intrigued, so I tried it and made it my own—of course, with a few modifications.

This recipe is in a couple of steps. It's not difficult, but there are a lot of things to do to get it done.

Tools

Two 12-inch dutch ovens, charcoals vary with the step

Ingredients

8–10 small to medium potatoes
1/4 cup milk
3 Tbsp. butter
salt and pepper
1 1/2 to 2 lbs. ground beef (could substitute lamb, if you can find it)

1 cup beef broth
1/4 cup flour
two large carrots
one large onion
1 Tbsp. minced garlic
1 cup sliced mushrooms
liberal shakes of Worcestershire sauce
Liberal shakes of parsley, rosemary, and oregano
Liberal shakes of salt and black pepper

I started with a lot of coals, maybe 20 or so, underneath each of two 12-inch dutch ovens. In one were the potatoes, peeled and cubed. In the other was the ground beef, browning. Actually, I ended up putting more coals on top of the potatoes as well. You want to get it good and boiling.

Once both were done, I brought them inside (it was cold outside) and drained the potatoes. I added the milk, butter, salt, and pepper and mashed them with a whisk.

Then I put them in the fridge next to the meat. I cleaned up the ovens and went to church.

When I got home, I put the meat in one of the 12-inch dutch ovens and added everything else on the ingredient list. The original recipe instructions called for sautéing the onions, garlic, mushrooms, and carrots first and then adding the meat and broth, but by this time, I'd already taken a lot of steps to cook this and wanted to simplify it. So, I just dumped it all in with the meat and mixed it up.

Then, I spread the potatoes on top. I had not used this many potatoes, and in a 12-inch dutch oven, I couldn't completely cover the meat, so that's why the ingredients list has more. The book suggested dragging a fork through the potatoes to make a pattern, and I thought that was a pretty cool idea, so I tried it. It gives it a sort of "Zen garden" look!

Then, I put it on enough coals to make it about 350 degrees. Normally that's about 8–9 below and 16–18 above. I ended up with about 12 below and 22 above since it was winter. I left it there for about 40 minutes. Also, in an attempt to brown the top of the potatoes, after that, I put all the coals on top and let it cook for about another 20 minutes.

It tasted delicious! I loved the herbal flavor.

DUTCH OVEN CHALLENGES

My friend Andy, a fellow dutch ovener and erstwhile blogger, and I used to send each other cooking challenges. It was our way of spurring our creativity and nudging each other to have a good time cooking and inventing. We would start by listing off some confusing and disparate ingredients with some strange instructions and then seeing what sort of dishes we would each create based on the parameters. Here are a couple of the challenges, along with my results.

I would encourage you to accept any of these challenges yourself, and, when you've done your best, post the results in a comment at marksblackpot.com!

Apples and Oranges

"You can't compare apples to oranges!" So the saying goes.

Well, in this dutch oven challenge, we won't compare. Instead, we will combine.

I thought about these two fruits and how much I love the luscious flavors of each one. I started thinking how much I love to combine savory meats and sweet flavors together into the same dish. So, here's the challenge, open to any dutch oven chef.

Ingredients

Prepare a dish using the following ingredients:

apples (in any form)
oranges (in any form)
any meat (some kind of meat must be included)
mint (in any form)
other ingredients, such as spices and seasonings as you see fit

The dish should be as original as possible. Go to the 'net for ideas, if you wish, but try to make it your own. Let's see what we can come up with!

Here's my result.

Dutch Oven Orange and Apple Curried Pork Chops

Tools

12-inch dutch oven
15 coals below
20 coals above

Ingredients

4 cloves garlic, minced
2 medium onions, chopped
5–6 green onions, chopped
4–5 stalks celery, chopped
2 medium apples, cored and thinly
    sliced
1/4 cup fresh parsley, chopped

1/4 cup fresh mint, chopped
1 (14 oz.) can coconut milk
1 can full of water
1 can full of rice
salt
pepper

pork chops
kosher salt
curry powder

1 jar orange marmalade
zest of 1 orange
juice of 1 orange
cinnamon

I started out (after lighting up some coals) by chopping, slicing, and mincing all of the veggie ingredients and the apples. I mixed everything together in the dutch oven down to and including the pepper in the ingredients list. Pretty easy so far.

In the next set of ingredients, I had to make some choices. I wasn't sure if I wanted to put the curry directly on the meat or to include it in the glaze. In the end, I decided to put it on the meat. I rubbed the meat, both sides, with kosher salt and curry powder. Then I layered the pork chops over the veggies, rice, and liquid. I had about 8–9 actual chops, so I had to overlap them in a circle.

Finally, I mixed the marmalade, the zest, the juice, and the cinnamon into a glop and spooned it onto the meat.

I put the oven out on the coals. It cooked for about an hour to an hour and a half so that everything was nicely baked and the liquid was absorbed by the rice.

I served it up with a twist of orange and sprinkled it with more minced mint leaves.

In the end, it had an interesting flavor. The rice, and even the meat, had a rich creaminess that I'm sure came from the coconut milk. The spices gave it an interesting flavor, one I'd not tasted before, so it was neat to have something almost completely new.

ANOTHER DUTCH OVEN CHALLENGE

The ingredients for this one were beef for the meat; leeks, scallions, and green onions for the veggies; and cinnamon for the spice.

Of course, I undertook the challenge! The process confused me, and in many ways, until I actually did it, I wasn't sure what I was going to do. In my mind, I was going to make the beef and the onions and then do a dairy-based sauce with nutmeg and cinnamon. My main confusion was in how to handle the roux for the sauce. In the end, the process I chose worked, but I might do it differently if I ever do it again.

By the way, if any of you out there can come up with a good name for this dish, let me know, 'cause I'm stumped. For now, it's

That One Beef Dish That Mark Made for the Dutch Oven Challenge

Tools

12-inch dutch oven
a lot of coals under (for the first steps)
10 coals below
16 coals above (for the final steps)

Ingredients

2–3 Tbsp. oil
2–3 Tbsp. flour

2–3 cloves garlic
1 medium onion, diced

3 scallions/green onions, chopped
salt

1 lb. ground beef
pepper

2 large potatoes, quartered and sliced
1 sweet pepper, diced

2 cups milk
nutmeg
cinnamon
more flour, if necessary, to thicken

I started out by making the roux out of equal parts of oil and flour in the open dutch oven, with bottom heat only. For some reason, my coals were very slow lighting that day, and it took a while to make even the blondest of a blonde roux. It was also pretty runny.

Once the roux had cooked a bit and browned just a little, I added the second set of ingredients to sauté. I wasn't sure how well it would sauté with the roux still in the pot, but my friend Alton did it once, and it seemed to work, so I guessed it was okay. This was a large part of my aforementioned confusion.

Once the onions were translucent, I added the ground beef and let it brown.

When the beef was pretty much cooked through and all stirred up, I added the potatoes and sweet peppers. At this point, I covered the dutch oven and set up the coals for baking/roasting, with top and bottom heat, as listed on the opposite page. I let the potatoes cook a bit, stirring things occasionally.

When I could see that the potatoes were starting to cook but not completely done (maybe just a bit firmer than al dente), I poured in the milk. I didn't measure it but rather guestimated it. I poured it in until it came up halfway on the meat and potatoes. In other words, I did not completely cover the food with milk. There was enough milk that I could see it rising as I poured, but the level of the milk was nowhere near the top of the food. I stirred in the nutmeg and cinnamon and let it cook and simmer some more, covered, until the potatoes were done.

I did add a little more flour for a bit of thickening, but it didn't need much. In retrospect, I'd probably do more roux at the beginning.

I served it up on two slices of the artisan bread I'd made the day before from a dutch oven bread recipe I had. The tangy bread and the meat made a magnificent combination.

The taste was delicious, and my son pronounced it amazing. I'd say this challenge was a success. Any other takers?

CHAPTER 6

SIDE DISHES

BAKING, ROASTING, OR FRYING some meat or a fancy main dish is a vital part of the meal. It's the central focus. But the side dishes are, in many ways, just as important, if not more so. They are like the supporting cast of a great movie. If you only had the stars on the screen, there wouldn't be anyone to interact with, and no variety in the experience.

In addition, there are a few core culinary skills involved in making side dishes, such as cooking rice, steaming veggies, or baking potatoes.

RICE

When I was first getting started in dutch oven cooking, my (then) young son went shopping with my wife for my birthday present one year and picked out a cool little 8-inch dutch oven for me. At the time, I looked at it and thought, *That's really cute, but I'll never use it.*

I was so wrong.

One of the ways I use it the most is to make the rice for a side dish or curries or meats. The small dutch oven is also perfect for sauces and gravies.

Getting rice right can be tricky. You must have enough liquid, and you must cook the rice long enough to soften and absorb the liquid, but not so long that it burns on the bottom.

Tools

8-inch dutch oven
8–10 coals each above and below

Ingredients

2 cups water or, preferably, chicken broth
1 cup long grain white rice
salt

I put the rice and the stock into the small dutch oven and put it on the coals covered. Then, I watch for it to boil by seeing the steam venting out from under the lid. That tells me it's been boiling for a while. At that point, I just keep it on the coals for about another 10 minutes. Then I pull if off the coals and let it sit for a while longer with the lid on. Eventually, it stops venting and cools down. While this is happening, the rice is still cooking, still absorbing the liquid. If you lift the lid too much, the steam flies away, and you have less liquid to be absorbed by the rice. If you can cook it completely without ever lifting the lid, you've perfected the art of cooking rice in a dutch oven! Finally, when it's ready to serve, I'll open the lid and fluff it up with a fork.

I eventually learned that I could tell when the rice was done by sight. If the rice grain is translucent with no hard whiteness in the center, it's cooked through.

VEGGIE RICE

This is an elaboration on the basic plain rice side dish mentioned previously. It's full of other great flavors.

Ingredients

1/4 lb. smoked sausage, thin sliced
1 onion, sliced
2 Tbsp. minced garlic
2 sweet peppers (I used half each of red, yellow, orange, and green for color.)

1 jalapeno, seeded and sliced
4 green onions, sliced

1 cup rice
2 cups chicken stock
zest of 1 lemon
juice of 2 lemons
salt and pepper

Once the veggies are all chopped, I put the onions, garlic, and sausage in the oven and on the coals to brown. Once those are ready, I put in the veggies, rice, and stock. Then I add the lemon ingredients and the seasoning. I cover it and leave it on the coals (transferring some coals to the top) for about 20 minutes until the rice is done.

PARMESAN STEAMED VEGGIES

For a picture of this recipe, scan this QR code:

Tools

10-inch dutch oven
15–18 coals beneath

Ingredients

1 small head cauliflower

1 stem broccoli
2 peppers (preferably of different colors)
snow peas or green snap beans

2–3 cups water

Parmesan cheese
italian salad dressing.

One Sunday afternoon, as the turkey was nearing done, I got to thinking about what to serve as a veggie side. I suddenly got this idea to do an oven full of steamed mixed veggies. I cut a bunch of veggies of various kinds and colors into bite-size bits. I used snow peas, broccoli, red and yellow sweet peppers, and cauliflower. I put them on one of those metal, fold-out steamer things and added a few cups of water. That went out on the coals. Soon I could see the steam venting out from under the lid.

Unfortunately, the first few times you do this, you'll have to lift the lid from time to time and check on the veggies. Eventually, you'll get a feel for how long they take and you'll know better when to pull them off the heat. I would check after about 15–20 minutes and then every 10 minutes or so after that.

If they're done, they'll still be quite firm to your bite and rather crispy, but a little softer than when raw. The colors will have become vibrant and vivid.

When they were done, I pulled them out of the dutch oven and put them in a serving bowl. I poured some italian dressing over them and sprinkled on some more Parmesan cheese. Then I shook the bowl to toss them, and they were ready to serve! They were delicious and elegant.

ZEN ON THE COB IN THE DUTCH OVEN

For a picture of this recipe, scan this QR code:

Tools

10-inch dutch oven
15–18 coals beneath

Ingredients

3–4 corn cobs
2–3 cups water

Spicy Steamed Corn on the cob
1/2 cup (1 stick) softened butter
Salt
Garlic powder
Black pepper
Paprika
Cayenne powder (very little, to
taste)

From My Blog

"I like fancy. I like complex. I like a challenge. I like to see if I can pull off intricate dishes and stretch myself. I like to take simple dishes and enhance them, to kick them up a notch.

"This weekend, however, I got to cook something incredibly simple. And it tasted wonderful.

"We were having a big barbecue party for a lot of Jacob's teachers and support staff at the school, and I spent a lot of time at the grill—naturally. But on the side, I made some steamed corn on the cob.

"I started by lighting a lot of coals and pouring about half of them (I'm guessing about 20 or more) onto my cooking surface. I put a veggie steamer (one of those metal fan-out things) in the bottom of my 12-inch-deep dutch oven. I poured in water until it was just up to the level of the steamer and laid the corn cobs (shucked and snapped in half) on it. Then I put the dutch oven on the coals.

"Pretty soon, it was venting steam a little, so I knew it was boiling. I kept fresh coals on it for about 30–45 minutes, just until the corn looked yellow and cooked (like corn on the cob is supposed to look when it's ready to eat). Then we served it with butter, salt, and pepper. Yum! Only two pieces were left over when the party was done.

"Sometimes, simple and pure is perfect, right?

"If you want to mess with perfection and tweak up the corn recipe above, mix up the spices and butter before you cook. Let it sit for a while to absorb all the flavors. When the corn is done, just smear it on, melting it all over the corn, and it will be amazing!"

POTATOES

Simple Baked Potatoes (with foil)

Tools

10-inch dutch oven (2–4 servings)
6–8 coals below
12–16 coals above

Ingredients

12-inch dutch oven (4–8 servings)
8–10 coals below
16–18 coals above
2–8 medium potatoes (one per diner)

Toppings at serving

salt
pepper
butter
sour cream
fresh chives/green onions
bacon crumbles
grated cheddar
chilli
cheese sauce

To start off, while my coals are getting hot (and usually while the other dishes of the dinner are cooking), I'll thoroughly clean the potato skins, making sure to scrub off any residual dirt. Then, I wrap each potato in a square of aluminum foil. I make sure that the shiny side of the foil is facing inward, toward the potato, to reflect heat back in rather than reflect it away from the potato. Then I use a fork or pointed knife to poke holes in the potatoes to help vent the steam from the liquid inside.

Then, simply put the potatoes in the dutch oven, and put the oven on the coals. It'll bake a while, about an hour, especially if you have more potatoes. When you can pierce the potato easily with a fork, with little resistance, it's done.

The foil will help steam the potatoes and also help keep them warm before serving. When you serve them, you can put on any toppings you like. If you do a big selection of toppings, you can even make the potatoes into a main dish and let the diners dress them as they please from a toppings bar.

Slightly Fancier Baked Potatoes
(without foil)

Tools

10-inch dutch oven (2–4 servings)
6–8 coals below
12–16 coals above

12-inch dutch oven (4–8 servings)
8–10 coals below
16–18 coals above

Ingredients

2–8 medium potatoes (one per diner)
olive oil
2 Tbsp. kosher salt
2 Tbsp. black pepper
2 Tbsp. paprika

Toppings at serving

salt
pepper
butter
sour cream
fresh chives/green onions
bacon crumbles
grated cheddar
chilli
cheese sauce

This is one of my preferred methods for baked potatoes. It's a lot more like some of the restaurants do, and it makes delicious and slightly crispy potatoes. We're not going to use foil, because the cast iron will trap the steam and keep it warm after cooking anyway, and we're going to season the skin.

Just like before, when the rest of the meal cooking is underway, I'll clean each potato and dry it off with a paper towel. I'll poke holes in each potato with a fork or knife.

Next, I'll mix the salt, pepper, and paprika together in a bowl. Then I'm ready to prep the potatoes. One by one, I'll use a basting brush to coat the potato skin with olive oil. I do it liberally. Then, I liberally sprinkle it with the mixed seasonings to coat it. I put the potatoes into a dutch oven that has been lightly oiled. It's okay to stack them if you have to. It's not absolutely necessary, but if the dutch oven has been preheated, the cooking time will be less. Also, if you have to mix up more seasonings, that's fine.

I set the dutch oven on the coals (if it's not already preheated). I'm careful not to jostle it around too much or to stir them up, because I want the seasonings to stick to the skin and not scrape off until the potato is cooked.

In about an hour or so, the potato will be soft, and I can pierce it easily with a knife or fork. I carefully lift them out, and they have a delicious spicy skin crust on them.

Even Fancier Baked Potatoes

Tools

12-inch dutch oven
8–10 coals below
16–18 coals above

Ingredients

4–5 medium to large potatoes
4–5 cloves garlic
olive oil
kosher salt
sesame seeds

This method of doing baked potatoes is visually cool and very tasty. The extra work in presentation makes a huge difference on the plate! It's not hard to do, but it does take a little time.

Step one is to peel the garlic and slice it into thin slivers. Then I wash, rinse, and dry the potatoes. I slice them almost all the way through in narrow rows so they can fan open a little. Then, in every other slice or so, I insert a sliver of garlic. I alternate between the middle and the right and left sides so that the slices of the potatoes will separate in different and unique ways. Really, it's tough to describe this process. It's better to look at the picture. As each potato is sliced, and the garlic has been inserted into it, I put it into the dutch oven.

Once all the potatoes are prepped, I drizzle each one with a bit of olive oil and sprinkle them with kosher salt and sesame seeds. It really makes for an impressive display. I put them in the oven and on the coals to bake.

Because they've been sliced, they don't take as long to cook as a solid baked potato—maybe 40 minutes or so. When they're done, I carefully lift them from the oven onto the plates. It really dresses up the dinner!

Dry Roasted Potatoes

This side dish is a bit of a favorite of mine and is easy to set up. It cooks the potatoes with a bit of a crispy edge, and the seasonings are delicious. It uses my dry-roasting technique, where you lift the lid a bit to let the steam out. Here's how I did it the first time I tried it.

Tools

12-inch dutch oven
25 + coals each above and below, for
    dry-roasting

Ingredients

4–5 medium to large potatoes
olive oil
parsley
salt
pepper
1–2 cloves of garlic, minced

I started out by lighting the fire. This was a bit of a challenge because of how windy as it was, but eventually I had coals getting white. While they were heating up, I cleaned the potatoes. I had originally thought about doing this with baby potatoes. That would have been yummy. But I didn't have any. So, I used regular potatoes, quartered and sliced in cube-like chunks.

I put them in a bowl and dashed some olive oil on them. Then I added all the other seasonings and flavorings. I shook the bowl to mix them all up.

Then I went out and put the oven on the coals to preheat. I spritzed a little extra oil in the bottom. Once the oven was a bit hot, I put in the potatoes.

Then, I set the lid up for the dry roast. This is done by putting something over the edge of the pot, under the lid, to lift the lid of the dutch oven and let the steam out. A long, heavy-gauge wire (like a coat hanger) reaching across the top of the dutch oven would work nicely. That same wire, or a nail that's bent into a U shape and hooked over the edge of the dutch oven is good too. If you use the nail though, make sure it doesn't fall into the food and get lost!

Since you're letting the steam and the hot air escape (it's normally trapped under the heavy lid), you have to use a lot more coals. (See the previous page.)

I let the potatoes cook for a while, using the dry-roasting technique, until they were seared on all sides and the seasonings were clinging to them. Since I was fighting the temperature, it took a little longer, but I think in normal conditions, it should take 30–40 minutes or so, with a couple of stirrings.

Au Gratin Potatoes

For a picture of this recipe, scan this QR code:

I often cook our Christmas dinner in the dutch ovens. Cold or not, it's fun and delicious. I cook most of the morning and serve it up as sort of a late lunch or early dinner at about three o'clock. One year, I did au gratin potatoes for one of the sides.

Tools

12-inch dutch oven
15–20 coals below to fry the bacon and create the roux
12 coals each above and below to sauté the onions and
veggies and cook the potatoes and dairy ingredients

Ingredients

1 lb. bacon
flour to make a roux

1–2 medium onions, diced
3 cloves garlic, minced

4–5 medium potatoes, quartered and
sliced

1 pint of cream
1 cup milk

salt
pepper

1–2 handfuls grated cheddar cheese
fresh parsley

a little more cheese

I had actually done au gratins a time or two before, using different recipes and processes, but this time was the most successful. As an overview of the steps, the first is to crispy fry some bacon pieces and then use the resulting grease to make a roux. Then you sauté some onions and veggies and finally add the potatoes and the dairy.

Here are the details.

First, I took a package of bacon and cut it into 1-inch squares. I put the bacon in a dutch oven over some hot coals and set it frying. It took a while, because I wanted them to be nicely crisp. (Crisper, even, than I like it for breakfast.)

Once that was done, I pulled out the bacon and also a little bit of the grease. I added flour, a tablespoon at a time, to the remaining grease in the pot to make a roux. I added it slowly, because I was looking for a particular consistency. I wanted it to be a little softer than cookie dough. I think I used about a half cup. I stirred it to cook it a bit, but not too much. I still wanted a lighter roux. When that was ready, I pulled it out. That was, of course, way more roux than I would need for the dish, but that's okay. It's nice to have extra when you need it. It keeps in the fridge for quite a while.

While the bacon and the roux were cooking, I cut up the potatoes, quartering them and slicing the pieces to 1/4 inch. That makes them easier to spoon up and eat, and they'll cook quicker and more consistently.

Then, I reheated the extra bit of reserved grease and threw in the onions and the garlic to sauté.

Once those were nice and brown, I added in the bacon, the potatoes, and the cream. I added the milk, because I was out of cream and still felt it needed more liquid. If you have enough half and half, just use that. Then I added the salt and pepper. I was liberal with those, too.

I let it all cook for a bit until the potatoes just started to get soft (sort of an al dente feel). Then, I opened it up and added the roux, about a tablespoon at a time. I stirred it in and continued to stir it for a few moments while I watched the consistency change. If you just start dropping in the roux, you'll probably add too much, and it will get too thick. I kept adding it until it felt like a sauce or a thick gravy instead of a milky liquid.

Once the potatoes felt pretty much done, I added the cheese and the parsley. Stir it all in, and it will get nice and gooey. The roux will keep the cheese melty instead of all clumpy and coagulated. (When that happens, they say it breaks.) The final step is to add a layer of cheese to the top and let it melt. At that point, you can take it off the coals altogether and let the residual heat in the dutch oven melt the cheese.

Serve it up!

CHAPTER 7

DESSERTS

COOKING IS WHEN YOU TAKE FOOD INGREDIENTS and run them through a process (usually involving heat) and end up with something that's a delicious combination of the flavors and textures of the ingredients that have been altered by the process.

The reason I mention this is that many cookbooks tend to neglect (or assume that you already know) the process part. They list the ingredients, and using an arcane shorthand, briefly describe the process.

Well, as I was learning how to do desserts (and failing miserably at it along the way), I started to see just how important it is to know and follow the process. That's where the magic lies! That's what transforms your simple flour, sugar, and butter into something light and fluffy.

And if you don't think a cake can be magic, just look at a kid's face on his or her birthday, all lit by smiles and candlelight!

CAKES

A SIMPLE DUTCH OVEN YELLOW LAYER CAKE

For a picture of this recipe, scan this QR code:

I'm a little weird in the dutch oven community. So many have what they call *castironitis*, which is mostly a financial disorder. It's main symptom is an impulse to own lots of dutch ovens, whether or not you actually use them.

So far, I've not been infected with it. I've only have about a dozen pieces of cast iron cookware. (Trust me, that's a small collection!) Still, once in a while, I find that I need a new dutch oven for one reason or another.

I hadn't bought a new one in a long time, mostly because I hadn't needed a new one. I've seen quite a few that I liked a lot and wanted to buy, but I never really *needed* them. There are those, true, who would argue that you don't actually have to *need* or even *use* all of the cast iron you acquire.* But, for me, to spend the money, I have to need it. And the need and the money never came together at the right moment.

But . . .

I'd been wanting to get good at baking dutch oven cakes, and I really think that cakes do better in 10-inch dutch ovens. You can do one in a 12-inch oven, but the recipes are usually designed for a 9-inch circle, which will make just the right amount for a 10-inch oven. So, if you do it in a 12-inch oven, it will be thinner, bake out faster, and end up a bit drier. Just not as good.

That's all well and good. I have a wonderful 10-inch dutch oven. Why buy another one? For one reason, if I want to do a layer cake (which is mostly what I like), then I'll want to bake them both at the same time. Otherwise, I'll end up mixing the batter twice and baking it twice, and it will be twice the work and twice the time. Not acceptable.

So, I needed a second 10-inch dutch oven.

Well, I bought it and brought it home. Excited, I found a chocolate cake recipe and tried it.

Failed!

I was not impressed. My family thought it was pretty good, but I thought it was dry, which seemed to be a common problem with my cakes. I mean, it wasn't an epic failure, but it just didn't make me say, "Wow! That's good!"

Part of the problem was that it was a tricky recipe, and I wasn't sure of the process, so it just didn't turn out very well. So, undaunted, I tried again. I picked a simpler recipe, learned the process, and baked it up. It was great! Victory! I put this recipe in here as the first cake in the chapter so I can refer to it and help show the real process of making a great cake.

Keep in mind as you're doing this recipe that it was doubled for two layers. If you're only doing one layer, half it back down.

Tools

Two 10-inch dutch ovens
10 coals below
18 coals above

Batter
Ingredients

3 cups white sugar
1 cup + 2–3 Tbsp. butter at room
  temperature
6 eggs

4 cups cake flour
3 tsp. baking powder
2 tsp. salt
1 tsp. ground cinnamon
1 tsp. ground nutmeg

2 cups milk
2 tsp. vanilla extract

Frosting

Ingredients

8 Tbsp. butter

4 Tbsp. cocoa

3 cups confectioners sugar, plus extra, if needed

4 Tbsp. milk

2 tsp. vanilla

I have learned, by the way, that process is as important—if not more so—as the ingredients. First, I gathered the ingredients, particularly the milk, eggs, and butter, and set them out on my counter to reach the ambient temperature. After letting them sit for a few hours, I got the party started by putting the coals on to burn and get all white and glowy.

I have to preface this description of the process by saying that I debated in my own mind how to work the ingredients. In the dutch oven world, particularly in IDOS-sanctioned, WCCO-qualifying cook-offs, it's against the rules to use any electrical equipment. That's right, no blenders, no mixers—nuthin'. Use your arms or go home.

My wife razzes me about this. While I was making this cake, for example, I was working the butter and the sugar, and she leaned over and whispered, "You know we have a mixer, don't you?"

Well, I'd decided to learn how to do it without electricity to make it compliant with the cook-off rules. Even though I might not ever win a cook-off with it, someone out there reading this might. In the meantime, if you want to use something you plug into a wall or something that has batteries, I won't stop you or turn you in to the cast iron police. Go for it.

Once everything was at room temperature (I even partially melted the butter), I mixed the butter and sugar together. Using the back of a slotted spoon, I creamed them together. By that, I mean that I quickly worked the spoon, mashing the sugar and butter together. I did this for a long time. After a time, it got a bit frothy and became easy to work with. The idea was to infuse it with air bubbles. Then, one at a time, I added the eggs, creaming and working the batter more between each addition.

Once that was well blended, I turned my attention to the next set of ingredients. I sifted the dry ingredients all together into a separate mixing bowl. (Sifting not only works out chunks, but it also blends the ingredients well and aerates the flour. More trapped air!) I also added the vanilla to the milk and stirred them together.

Now, I had three sets of ingredients, and it was almost time to blend them all together. First, however, I prepared the dutch ovens. I took the lids out to the cooking area and shook out a lot of coals onto each one so that each lid could preheat. Then, I sprayed the insides of the dutch ovens with oil and dusted them with flour, concentrating on the sides of the ovens. For the bottoms, I cut two 10-inch circles of parchment and placed them in the ovens. The oil helped hold them in place. I've tried to remove cakes from dutch ovens without the parchment and it's very difficult, even with the pan oiled and floured.

I added half of the flour mix and half of the milk to the butter-egg blend and mixed them together with a hand-crank egg beater. After they were well blended and aerated, I added the remainder and mixed them in well too. I mixed it for a total of 3–4 minutes. It wore me out. In the process, I also tried a whisk, and even the slotted spoon. I'm not sure which I liked best, but I think it was the cranker. It made it the smoothest.

Finally, it was ready. I poured it, 50–50, into each dutch oven. I arranged the coals and put the hot lids on the cakes. I marked the time. The reason you want to preheat the lid is so that there's a blast of heat to immediately bloom up all of those air bubbles you've strained so hard to make in all the previous steps. Without that, the cake will come out more dense and less fluffy.

Then I rested! I think during the mixing phase I worked off enough calories to eat the entire cake!

After 15 minutes or so, I turned the dutch oven and the lid. I was very careful not to jar or jolt it in case it would fall. The last time I baked, I wasn't so careful and had a sunken middle.

After 25 minutes baking, I checked for doneness. I did the toothpick trick, sticking it in and pulling it out dry. One of the cakes passed the test but was obviously not done. (It was still jiggly in the middle.) So, you have to be careful and observant as well. I ended up leaving them on the coals for around 35–45 minutes. One of my 10-inch dutch ovens is a deep one, and it took about 5–10 minutes longer to bake.

As each one was done, I brought it inside and took off the lid. I let it cool completely in the dutch oven before I attempted the removal.

In the meantime, I mixed up the frosting and put it in the fridge. I also cut a 10-inch circle out of a corrugated cardboard box.

When the cake was cool, I put the disc of cardboard on top of the cake and flipped the dutch oven over. The parchment let the cake drop right out with no issues at all. I peeled off the parchment and placed an inverted cake plate on top of the cake. Finally, I flipped it over, and there was my first layer. Voila!

I trimmed the first layer to be more flat and spread the frosting over the top of it. I extracted the second layer the same way, but I used my hand instead of the plate to invert the cake gently into position on the first layer. Once that was in place, I frosted the top and the sides and put it in the fridge until serving time.

When it was all done, it was moist and delicious! Definitely a hit!

For a video of this recipe, scan this QR code:

*There will be no comments on the size or scope of my magic: the gathering card collection. That's totally different.

SPICE CAKE

I remember my oldest son's fifteenth birthday, and, of course, a prime opportunity for me to show off my newfound cake-baking skills. I knew he didn't like chocolate cakes. (I don't know what his problem is, but I love him and accept him anyway.) So, I asked him what he wanted. His answer was pretty quick: a spice cake.

That was cool with me, 'cause I love my spices!

I looked all over for a good recipe, and I found many. Many required buttermilk. That's fine, but I didn't have any. The following recipe contains elements of several that I found that used vinegar for the acid to react with the soda instead of the buttermilk.

This time, I didn't make my own frosting. Shame on me!

This recipe makes enough for a two-layer cake.

Tools

Two 10-inch dutch ovens
8–9 coals below
12–14 coals above

Ingredients

2 1/2 cups cake flour
2 tsp. baking powder
1/2 tsp. baking soda
1 tsp. ground nutmeg
1 tsp. ground cinnamon
1 tsp. ground ginger
1/2 tsp. ground cloves
1/2 tsp. allspice
1/2 tsp. salt

1 1/2 sticks butter (softened)
1 1/2 cups light brown sugar

4 eggs

1 cup milk
1 tsp. white vinegar

A few hours before you start, take everything you need out of the fridge to warm up. It will work much better if it's all at ambient temperature instead of cold.

I started by sifting and mixing all of the dry ingredients together. You can whisk it together or mix it however you want. I use a flour sifter. The sifter helps aerate the flour, as well as blend the ingredients. I set the dry ingredients aside in a bowl.

After that, I went outside and lit up the coals I would need. I knew I'd need a lot of coals, because I was going to be baking two ovens at once. I also should have taken measures to make sure that my metal dutch oven table was level. More on that in a minute.

The next step is to cream the butter and sugar. I used a metal slotted spoon. I've also used a potato masher. A fork with long tines can work as well.

So, I creamed the butter and sugar together. Not only is it much easier if the butter is warm and soft, but it also accepts the air a bit better, which is really the whole point of this. It takes a long time to whip it up into a froth with only a slotted spoon. If you want to, you can use a tabletop blender or a hand beater. Of course, if you're out in the woods, you can't plug anything in, so you're back to the slotted spoon or the potato masher. I worked at it for a good 15 minutes or more.

Then I prepared the dutch ovens. I took the lids out to the coals and poured a bunch of hot, white coals on each one and set them aside on the dutch oven table to preheat. I cut a disc of parchment paper to fit the bottom of each oven and held it in place by spraying oil on the bottom first. I did all this preparation first, since once I start mixing the wet ingredients, I don't want to stop.

I added the eggs to the butter-sugar mixture, one at a time, and beat it all together with the slotted spoon until each one was well blended. Then I added in a third of the dry ingredients and blended them in (with a stiff wire whisk this time), followed by about half of the milk. (I also added the vinegar at this point.) I added another third of the powders and then the last half of the milk. At each stage I paused to whisk it all in well. A few good final whisks, and it was finally a beautiful, creamy, fluffy batter. The spices made it smell amazing too. It's tough not to eat it like this. Fortunately, as the chef, I get to lick the mixing spoon!

I poured it into each dutch oven, a spoonful or two at a time, to make sure it was even between the two. I immediately took it out and set the coals in their proper order (as listed above). By the way, here's an interesting note. One of my 10-inch dutch ovens is deep, and the other is shallow. I've learned that I need to put a couple of extra coals on top of the deep one.

I left it to bake. After about 10–15 minutes, I turned the oven and the lid to prevent hot spots. Be careful doing this! If you jar your oven, you can make the cake collapse. I know. I've done it.

After 25–30 minutes, test the center of the cake with a toothpick. If it comes out clean, leave it in for a couple minutes longer and then take it off the coals.

Once both cakes were done, I brought them inside and let them cool in the dutch ovens with the lids off. When they're cool, I run a knife around the perimeter of the cake to loosen it (if it's not already—cooling usually pulls it away from the sides), and then invert it onto a small plate or a cardboard disc.

Finally, I stacked and frosted them. They were delicious! Happy birthday to him!

ZEBRA CAKE

For a picture of this recipe, scan this QR code:

The first time I made this cake, which was a long time ago, was for my wife's birthday, but I'd done it with boxed cake mixes. The basic idea is to make a white and a chocolate cake mix, marble and swirl the two mixes together, and decorate it as a layer cake. Here, you'll find the recipe to do it all from scratch.

Sort of . . .

When digging through our family recipes, I found this series of pages all about making your own basic mixes and storing them for when you want to bake. So, this recipe is from a mix that was made from scratch!

My first step was to mix up the mix!

Basic Cake Mix

Ingredients

10 1/2 cups flour
1/3 cup baking powder
8 cups sugar
1/2 cup cornstarch
1 Tbsp. salt
4 cups shortening

I started by measuring out the flour into a sifter and sifting it into the bowl. I actually used cake flour. I did get a really fluffy crumb on the cake, and the cake flour might have been one of the reasons why. Then I mixed in the rest of the dry ingredients. Finally, I cut in the shortening with a pastry-blending knife. Once the shortening was pretty well blended, I mixed it more with my hands. Finally, I put it in a large zip-top bag and labeled it.

Cakes

Tools

Two 12-inch dutch ovens
10 coals below
18 coals above

Once the mix was made, I started a lot of coals. I was going to need at least 60 for both ovens. It took a while for them to all start and become a uniform white. I staggered mixing the cakes with checking on the coals. Once they got white, I put 25+ coals on each dutch oven lid to preheat them and brought the dutch ovens in to the prep counter.

I got out two bowls for the cake mixing.

White Cake
Ingredients

3 1/3 cups basic cake mix

3 egg whites

1 cup milk

1 tsp. vanilla

This one was a pretty straightforward mix. I just combined the ingredients and beat them with a hand-crank egg beater. The egg yolks were discarded.

Chocolate Cake
Ingredients

9 Tbsp. cocoa

2 1/2 Tbsp. butter

3 1/3 cups basic cake mix

2 eggs

1 cup milk

For the chocolate, I mixed the butter and cocoa powder together first, creaming them together with the back of a slotted spoon, and then I added them into the other ingredients. Again, I mixed it with a hand-crank egg beater until it was smooth.

I noticed that the white cake was considerably thicker than the chocolate, so I added more milk to even the consistency. The recipe above reflects that added milk. You might still have to adjust one or the other.

I sprayed the bottom and sides of each dutch oven with cooking oil spray and sprinkled some flour liberally across the oil. I also cut out a circle of parchment paper and laid it across the bottom of both ovens. Getting the cake out is a bit of a challenge without it.

I got two big serving spoons, and one spoonful at a time, I added a bit of white cake mix, then a bit of chocolate, into each dutch oven. I continued alternating until both mixing bowls were empty. Then I took a spoon and swirled around through the mix. I took care not to stir or mix it. My effort was to simply swirl it. One or two passes through, no more.

I took the dutch ovens out to the coals and put the heated lids on, adjusting the coals for heat above and below.

While the cakes baked, I cut a couple of 12-inch discs of cardboard out of some empty boxes in my garage. These would help me extract the cakes.

The cakes themselves only took about 25 minutes to bake. I used the old toothpick method to determine doneness. You simply stick in the toothpick, and if it pulls out clean with no batter, it's done. Be careful, because cooking them too long can dry them out. These cakes were baked in 12-inch dutch ovens, so the cakes were a little thinner and cooked a little faster than in a 10-inch.

Once they were brought inside, I set them aside to cool. Then, I ran a spatula between the cake and the sides of the dutch ovens to separate them. I put one of the cardboard discs on top of each dutch oven and flipped it over, turning the cake onto the cardboard disc. Then I inverted it back onto a cooking rack. The parchment made that part easier as well. I did this with both dutch ovens.

Then it was just a matter of decorating the cake. We used chocolate and buttercream frosting for the zebra stripes. I let my son and a couple of neighborhood girls (who are definitely *not* his girlfriends, right?) handle the icing and decorating. I think they did a good job!

BLUEBERRY PANCAKE CAKE

For a picture of this recipe, scan this QR code:

I had a good idea not long ago. It seemed to me that a stack of pancakes looked a lot like a layer cake with lots of layers. From there, it was an easy set of mental leaps to make it into an actual dessert cake.

This recipe is in two parts: the pancakes and the frosting. The pancakes I took from my first book, *The Best of the Black Pot*, and I used blueberries instead of apples.

Blueberry Cinnamon Pancakes on the Dutch Oven lid

Tools

12-inch dutch oven lid, inverted on a trivet
20 coals underneath, with more in a side fire

Ingredients

3 cups flour
1 1/2 Tbsp. baking powder
1 tsp. salt
3 Tbsp. white sugar

2 1/2 cups milk, with as much as an additional cup to the side

2 eggs
6 Tbsp. butter, melted
1 cup of fresh blueberries, coarsely chopped (also set a few whole ones aside)
1–2 tsp. cinnamon
1 tsp. nutmeg

First, I made the pancakes. I started by lighting up the coals and getting them hot. Once they were ready, I put the trivet over the coals and the 12-inch dutch oven lid upside down on the trivet. I sprayed a little oil on the lid as it preheated.

In a bowl, I sifted and mixed the dry ingredients. I mixed in the wet ingredients and stirred them all up. I chopped up the berries (it wasn't easy since they kept rolling everywhere) and stirred them in along with the spices.

I find that pancakes cook better if the batter is runny. I added milk until it was the consistency I like. It's a little runnier than a typical cake batter.

Once it was all mixed up and the lid was heated up, I just started cooking the pancakes. I did a little less than a cup of batter for each one. I let it cook on one side until the bubbles would pop and not refill back in. Then, I'd turn it over for just a few moments more. This mix was enough for 6–7 of these big pancakes. When they were done, I brought them in and let them cool.

Then, it was time to mix up the frosting and assemble the cake.

Frosting
Ingredients

3 cups confectioners sugar
1 cup butter or cream cheese
1 tsp. vanilla extract
1 to 2 Tbsp. whipping cream

This is a particularly challenging part of the dish if you don't use any electrical appliances. Because IDOS cook-off rules currently forbid them, I like to do all of my blog dishes using hand tools. In this case, I recommend starting by creaming the butter or the cream cheese using the back of a spoon with holes in it, or a potato masher that has a flat plane with holes. Gradually add in the sugar to avoid making the batter too stiff right away. Then, when it starts to look good and aerated, mix in the vanilla and the whipping cream.

Once it's mixed, it's pretty easy to assemble. First, I took out about a third of the frosting for the top of the cake. Then, I started with one pancake on my plate and spread a paper-thin layer of frosting on it. I allowed a little more thickness at the edges, but not much. I also spread the frosting all the way to the edge. Then, I put another pancake on top of that.

Layer after layer—frosting, pancake, frosting—I built it up. It's important to not use too much frosting in between layers. Use less than a normal layer cake. First of all, you've got six or seven layers to frost, and it will get used up pretty fast. Second, six or seven full layers of frosting in the cake will make it pretty dang sugary!

Sometimes, the frosting would squeeze out a little from between the pancake layers. I didn't mind that. I thought it looked more cake-like that way.

Finally, after seven layers of cake, I'd pretty much used up my allotted two-thirds of the frosting. I plopped the final third on top and spread it around the top like a real frosting layer on cake should be. I pushed it all the way to the edge and even let it droop over a bit. I did not, however, frost the sides. My pancakes were not perfectly round, and I liked the irregularities of the edges. Finally, I judiciously sprinkled and scattered the few remaining unchopped blueberries across the top to get stuck in place by the frosting.

When serving, I cut it into wedges, just like a regular cake. The blueberries on top and the blueberries in the pancakes make for a delicious cake!

PIES

How to Make a Dutch Oven Pie Crust

I'm not a big pie baker. Not because I don't like them, of course, but because it takes a lot of work to do it right, and I'm still learning the process. Still, I love the results! I've made apple pies, pumpkin pies, and, most recently, a pecan pie.

One thing I've noticed as I'm baking is that the crust is pretty much the same process in each pie I bake. So, I'm thinking I should write that process separately, and then I can reference it in all of my pie recipes.

I used to make my pies in my 12-inch dutch oven, but over time, I discovered that the 10-inch is better. The 12-inch is usually too much pie, and some ends up being spoiled. So, 10-inch from now on.

Also, some people bake their pies in pie tins in a dutch oven. That does make it easier to craft and easier to lift out. However, current IDOS cook-off rules prohibit using any internal cooking devices, like pans or trivets, inside the dutch ovens. Plus, I really like baking right in the dutch oven. I also like serving from the dutch oven, so I'm not required to lift it out whole and complete. If you want to do that, it's not tough if you know the right tricks.

Tools

10-inch dutch oven
8–10 coals below
14–16 coals above

Pie Crust
Ingredients

1 1/4 cups shortening
3 cups flour
1 Tbsp. vinegar
5 Tbsp. water (chilled in ice)
1 egg

I start the crust by putting all of the ingredients into a large bowl. You can use butter or margarine, I'm told, instead of shortening, but they have other liquids in them, and they can make for less flaky crusts. I've always used all-purpose flour, because that's what I've had on hand. You can use pastry flour, if you want. It will have less protein, and so, less gluten.

I use a pastry cutter to mix the ingredients together. Blend them all but don't knead, since you don't want to build any gluten in the flour. Also, working it less with my hands keeps it cool so the fats don't melt.

Once it's mixed, I put it between two sheets of parchment or waxed paper and roll it. At this point, I'm not preparing it for the oven but rather creating layers so it can be rolled out quite thick. I dust it with a little flour, fold it in half, and then into quarters. Then, I roll it out again. A little more flour, fold, and more rolling. I do that process three to four times, creating layers in the stack. Then, I leave it in a clump, wrap it in plastic, and put it in the fridge to chill for a half hour or so.

In the meantime, I prepare the dutch oven. I lightly spray it with oil. Then, if I want to lift the pie out of the dutch oven when it's done, I prepare the lifting mechanism. I cut two big squares of parchment. I fold them into two long strips and lay them across the bottom of the dutch oven, folded up the sides and over the edges. Then I cut a circle of parchment (you can use the lid as a template and cut it just a little smaller) and lay that in the dutch oven, over the crossed strips of folded parchment.

For a picture of this process, scan this QR code:

Next, it's time to roll out the dough. I take it out of the fridge and break off about two-thirds of it. I put it between parchment or waxed paper sheets. I roll it out pretty thin and cut it just smaller than the dutch oven lid. I carefully lift the circle and the lower paper sheet and lightly fold it in half, with the paper on the inside. I set this down into the dutch oven and unfold the other half so that the entire bottom of the dutch oven is covered. Finally, I peel off the paper. It's tricky to position the dough after it's placed, so it's good to be careful with it as you put it in.

Then, I take all of the leftover dough from around the circle and the extra I broke away earlier, and I roll it out into a long rectangle. I cut that into strips, about an inch and a half wide and about a foot long.

Each of these strips are lifted up and placed around the inside sides of the dutch oven. I press them together and also press them down into the "corners" where the bottom of the dutch oven meets the wall of the dutch oven. Presto! The crust is in place. Once it's in place, take a fork and poke holes in the bottom and sides to vent the steam.

For a picture of this step, scan this QR code:

In most cases, it's now ready for the filling. Make the pie happen! (One tip I heard when making fruit pies is to spread softened butter over the interior of the pie to keep the crust from soaking up the liquid in the filling.)

If my pie has a top crust, I roll out another amount of dough and cut another circle about the size of the lid. Using the same technique, I lift it onto the filling and position it as I unfold it onto the top of the pie. I pinch the sides and the top crust together in a decorative way and cut stylish vent holes in the top (usually 3–4) so the steam can release and keep the crust from tenting.

Then, I brush the top of the crust with a little milk and sprinkle more sugar over the surface. This makes a nice, sweet glaze.

Now, in certain circumstances, it's a good idea to parbake the bottom crust (also known as prebaking or blind baking). If you're doing a custard pie, or a particularly wet fruit pie, or if the filling itself will not be baked (like a cream or mousse pie), this step is very important. This helps set the flakiness and crispness of the crust before the wet ingredients are baked. However, I can't think of a pie that might use a prebaked base with a top crust.

If I'm going to parbake, I light some coals (probably just before I start rolling out the dough) and let them get white-edged. Once the crust is assembled, I pour some dried beans into the bottom of the crust and spread them up the sides as well. This will help hold the crust down and prevent bubbling. I put the dutch oven out on the coals, as mentioned previously, and let it bake. Now, in a conventional kitchen in a preheated oven, a prebake will typically take about 10 minutes. In a dutch oven, you have to heat up the iron, so a partial bake should be about 20–25 minutes. If it's a cream pie or something that won't be baked, I fully bake it, about 30–35 minutes, until the sides are brown.

When it's done, I take it off the coals and let it cool. When I can handle it, I'll scoop out the beans with a spoon (or my fingers) and let the crust cool a little more.

At that point, the bottom crust is ready for pie!

Then, when the pie is all filled, baked, and cooled, you can lift the pie out of the dutch oven using the strips of parchment. It works best if there are two people lifting, each person lifting two ends, but I've done it successfully by myself.

BEAN AND COCOA PIE

For a picture of this recipe, scan this QR code:

   While I was working on my previous book, *Stop Drop and Cook*, which is all about cooking with food storage ingredients, I came across this idea of using beans as the substance for a custard pie. The thought struck me so oddly. *A bean pie? What on earth are they thinking?*

   But then, I thought about a recipe I'd heard of using mashed dark beans in brownies to lessen the oil content. My wife had made them a long time ago, and they were delicious. The beaniness didn't come through, and it had a very smooth feeling on my palate.

   So, why not in a pie?

   I mean, really, it's the same idea for a pumpkin pie. You make a custard with eggs and sugar and use pumpkin puree for the texture. You just use different spices, right? So, I decided to give it a try. But, as I was making it, I was careful not to tell my family what I was doing. If it flopped, I wanted to preserve plausible deniability!

   This version, I decided, would use non-emergency, non-shelf-stable ingredients. For the food storage recipe, get my book!

Tools

10-inch dutch oven
8–10 coals below
12–14 coals above

Crust

Ingredients

For crust ingredients and instructions, see page 113.

Filling

Ingredients

2 heaping cups mashed, cooked beans
2 1/2 cups sugar
2 Tbsp. molasses
3/4 cup butter
3 eggs
2 Tbsp. cocoa powder
nutmeg
mint leaves for garnish

   I tackled this pie in three steps. First, the beans; second, the crust; and finally, the rest of the filling.

   You can approach the beans in a few different ways. One is to bust open a couple of cans of refried beans (neutral ones, without any additional flavorings, like garlic, etc.). Another approach is to open a couple of cans of normal, unmashed beans. If you do this, I would recommend using two different kinds of beans for more protein.

The third approach is what I did, because, of course, I like more work. I mixed a half bag of dried black beans and a half bag of dried kidney beans into a bowl with a lot of water and let them soak overnight. Then, using the same 10-inch dutch oven with about 15 coals underneath, I simmered the beans until they were soft (which took a couple of hours).

In any case, once you've got some soft beans, you have to mash them. I tried this interesting device that looks like a saucepan with a smashing wedge on the inside attached to a crank. It didn't work. Maybe the holes on the bottom were too small, but it just didn't do it. So, I pulled all the beans back out and used a potato masher. If you do this, use one with a flat surface with holes instead of one with wavy, heavy wire. It will mash better. You can also use a slotted spoon.

Or, of course, you could use a blender. But, who wants to do that? That's too easy!

I made the pie crust in the 10-inch dutch oven according to the instructions on page 113. I recommend parbaking it.

So, at that point, I had the pie crust ready, the beans smooshed and ready, and some coals lit and heating up. It was time to make pie!

I started by smooshing the sugar, molasses, and butter together and creaming them. If you want to, you can use brown sugar, but I like adding my own molasses, because I can make it darker and richer if I want to. I creamed them all together until it started to get fluffy as tiny air bubbles started to incorporate into the mixture.

I added the eggs and blended them in, as well as blending in the other flavorings. Finally, I folded in the beans. Once they were folded in, I stirred the mixture aggressively to make sure everything was well incorporated.

I poured the mix into the waiting pie crust in the 10-inch dutch oven and set it on the coals. I baked it, covered, for 45 minutes or so. I don't trust the toothpick method when testing the doneness of pies. It works okay for cakes, but I've seen times when the toothpick came up clean and the filling was still runny in the middle. I look for jiggle and touch for resistance instead of toothpicking. Make sure, also, that you turn the dutch oven and rotate the lid every 15 minutes or so of baking so you don't have hot spots burning parts of your pie. Also, with a long cook time like that, you'll want to have a side fire going so you can replenish your coals as needed.

When it was all done, I took it off the coals and let it cool with the lid off. I like to serve it right out of the dutch, but if you're going to lift it, make sure it has fully cooled so that the crust is fully set.

I was pleasantly surprised with the flavor of the pie. My wife said she was amazed, and my kids liked it, too. Who knew beans could be dessert?

PECAN DATE PIE

For a picture of this recipe, scan this QR code:

I've always loved pecan pie, but I've never made it, and I had no idea how. But then, I figured I'd just do what I always do, which is looking up some recipes and blending the coolest ideas into one. I also talked with my dear sister, who gave me some really good ideas as well. Her biggest idea was to add the dates. She said that it gives some substance to the custard, even though they essentially dissolve in the cooking process.

She also suggested I try the dark syrup rather than the light.

Both ideas were spot on and turned into the best pecan pie I have ever eaten.

I also learned from one big mistake. Don't buy pecans in the shell. I like to cook from scratch as much as possible, and sometimes that leads me to do some pretty stupid things—such as staying up past midnight, shelling enough pecans to make a pie the next day. Not only was I exhausted, but my fingers were also cramped. Don't be like me. Buy them shelled. Your hands will thank you.

Tools

10-inch dutch oven
8–10 coals below
14–16 coals above

Crust
Ingredients

For crust ingredients and instructions, see page 113.

Filling
Ingredients

1/2 lbs. dried beans to weigh down the crust while parbaking
1 stick unsalted butter
1 cup packed light brown sugar
3/4 cup dark corn syrup
2 tsp. pure vanilla extract
1/2 tsp. grated orange zest (or about half the orange)
1/4 tsp. salt

3 large eggs
1/2 to 1 cup pitted and dried dates, coarsely chopped
2 cups pecan halves (1/2 pound)

For the process of making the pie crust, please see page 113. I would strongly recommend doing the parbaking. I did it this time, and it made a big difference, because the crust didn't soak up so much of the liquid of the filling. It was much more flaky.

I melted the butter over the coals that were still hot after parbaking the crust. I added the brown sugar and whisked it all together until it was melted and smooth. I took it off the heat and added in the corn syrup, stirring as I went. Then I added the rest of the ingredients, except the eggs, dates, and pecan halves.

The filling mixture was still hot at this point, so I was nervous about dumping in the eggs and having them curdle or scramble. So, I decided to temper them. I broke them into a separate bowl and whisked them to break them up and blend them together until they were smooth. Then, while whisking with one hand, I used my other hand to add tablespoonfuls of the hot mixture to the eggs. (The idea is to bring the temperature of the eggs up gradually so they don't cook at this point.) Finally, tablespoon after tablespoon, it felt like they were warm, and I poured the whole thing back into the mix.

Then I added the dates and pecans.

Finally, I poured all of it into the crust that was still in the 10-inch dutch oven.

I put the lid on and set the oven on fresh coals, as indicated previously, and baked it for about an hour, until it was clear that the filling was set in the center. I let it cool completely in the dutch oven.

This time, I chose to serve it from the dutch oven rather than try to lift it out. The crust, however, was durable and probably would have easily survived the lift. The pie was incredible, especially with whipped topping! My sister was definitely right about the dates.

SIMPLE DUTCH OVEN APPLE PIE

For a picture of this recipe, scan this QR code:

This recipe is from the blog, and it shows some of the things I was learning as I approached pie making. I remember my first ever attempt at making a pie—apple—and it was a disaster. The crust was weak, and the filling turned to mush. We don't talk about that one at my house. But with the mistakes comes the learning, right?

"Today was an odd day in a lot of ways. I've been stressed and down these last few days. Today, I was looking forward to attending a DOG (Dutch Oven Gathering) in Salt Lake City.

"But a major storm blew through. What a disappointment.

"Not the storm, mind. We need the wet here in Utah. The disappointment was that I couldn't go to the DOG. The storm was weird, too. It actually started snowing. In September! And we're not really that high up in elevation. The city of Eagle Mountain is in a valley, actually.

"But I was determined to cook something. I had originally planned on doing a pie, since I figured there'd be others there who would cook main dishes. So, I held to my plans. I used the last recipe I'd been successful with, but I'd been doing some research and thought I'd add a few things. So, I added the whipping cream and the nuts and raisins. It's cooling upstairs as I type.

Tools

12-inch oven
10 coals below
18 coals above

Crust

Ingredients
(I made two batches)

1 1/4 cups shortening
3 cups flour
1 Tbsp. vinegar
5 Tbsp. water
1 egg

Filling
Ingredients

6 apples, peeled and sliced
1 cup sugar
1 tsp. cinnamon
a shake or two of nutmeg
2 Tbsp. flour
1/2 cup chopped nuts
  (I used almonds)
1/4 cup raisins
1/2 pint (1 carton) heavy
  whipping cream

"I started off making the filling. I peeled and sliced the apples (they were kinda medium sized, so I did seven or eight). I probably coulda done one or two more and filled out the pie a little more. I cut the apples away from the cores and sliced them really thin. I put all the other ingredients in and stirred it up. This time, actually, I forgot the nutmeg. Bummer.

"Then I made the first batch of crust. I am not an expert crust maker by any means. This is the third time in my life I've made a pie, and I've never done it in a normal oven.

"I poured everything into a bowl and used a pastry cutter to mix it all up. They are hard on my wrists, but they work. I dumped the dough onto a couple of sheets of waxed paper, side by side, and layered more paper on top. Then I rolled it out. I used the dutch oven lid as a template and cut out a big circle.

"I have learned one cool trick. With the dough circle cut out, in between two layers of waxed paper, fold it in half. Then peel off the outer layer of waxed paper so there's sort of a crust "taco," a half circle with a folded sheet of waxed paper inside. Then lay it down on one side of the bottom of the dutch oven.

Finally, I flip the upper half of the crust over the other half of the dutch oven and peel off the waxed paper. That makes your bottom crust perfectly placed. Since it was cut from the lid, it'll be just a bit too big for the bottom. That's part of the plan. I formed it to the area where the base meets the side of the pot.

"I rolled out more dough and cut it into strips of about 2 to 2 1/2 inches wide (as long as the rolled-out dough was) and molded it onto the interior sides of the dutch oven, pressing it together with the base crust. I kept doing this until I had a nice wall all the way around the inside of the dutch oven."

(Author's Note: This crust process is essentially how it's described on page 113, with a few tweaks. One notable difference is that the crust and the filling in this recipe are designed for a 12-inch dutch oven when I usually, as I previously mentioned, do pies in a 10-inch oven now.)

"Then I poured in the filling.

"By this time, I was out of crust dough. So, I thought I'd better mix up more or there'd be none for the top. I rolled it out and played the same half-circle game to get the top crust placed.

"I cut out vent slices and used the pieces as decorative bits. I sprinkled milk on the top crust and sprinkled some cinnamon sugar on it.

"Then onto the coals for an hour or so, and it was done!"

OTHER GREAT DESSERTS

DUTCH OVEN BROWNIES

For a picture of this recipe, scan this QR code:

When I was working up the chocolate chicken recipe (see page 25), I decided to make it a whole chocolate day and do a great dessert too. My first thought was a chocolate cake, but I decided to make brownies instead. I looked up a good recipe, tweaked it a little, and here it is!

I've recently discovered just how much I like molasses as a flavoring. It not only sweetens, but it also adds depth and richness. I don't know how else to say that. I really like it.

Tools

10-inch dutch oven
9–10 coals below
18–22 coals above

Ingredients

soft butter, for greasing the pan
flour, for dusting the buttered pan

4 large eggs

2 cups sugar
1 Tbsp. molasses

8 ounces melted butter
1 1/4 cups cocoa
2 tsp. vanilla extract
1/2 cup flour, sifted
1/2 tsp. kosher salt
1 (16 oz.) bag chocolate chips

I started by lighting a lot of coals. While they were catching on fire, I broke the eggs into a bowl and whisked them. I beat them for a good 15 minutes or so until they were smooth, creamy, and a bit fluffy (a light yellow). I was surprised at how thick and airy the brownies ended up (airy for brownies, that is). I added the sugar and molasses and whisked them all together.

I got out the 10-inch shallow dutch oven and put 24 or so coals on the lid to preheat it. Then, I heavily buttered the base of the dutch oven and dusted it with flour. I was planning on cutting and serving the brownies directly from the dutch, so I didn't use any parchment paper. Had I been planning on extracting it as a disc, like a cake, I would have cut a parchment circle and put it down.

While the lid was heating, I added all of the remaining ingredients into the bowl and whisked and stirred some more. I worked it until it was smooth, which didn't really take long. I held back some of the chocolate chips for later.

I poured the batter into the dutch oven, took it out to the coals, and put the lid on. Then, I adjusted the coals to the numbers shown above and marked the time. After 15–20 minutes, I rotated the oven a quarter turn, and the lid as well, to prevent burns from hot spots. After another 15 to 20 minutes, I turned it again and lifted the lid to check on the progress. I checked it with a toothpick in the center. Almost done!

After about another 10 minutes, the toothpick came out clean, and I pulled it off the coals. I brought it in and let it cool, uncovered. It's tough, but I encourage you to resist the urge to eat it too quickly. Let it cool, at least until it's just barely warm. While it's still hot, scatter the remaining chocolate chips over the top and let the residual heat melt them. Another alternative topping is to sprinkle it with powdered sugar through a sifter.

We loved them! Especially after eating the chocolate chicken. A week or so later, my son cooked this up (increased for two 12-inch dutch ovens) at his Scout camp out and won his troop the Golden Spatula Award!

NUSSKUCHEN

For a picture of this recipe, scan this QR code:

 Nusskuchen (pronounced NOOS-COO-khen) is a German nut cake. In fact, it's a direct translation. *Nuss* means *nut*, and *kuchen* means *cake*. In our family, my mother made it every Christmas time. It's not for everyone, because it's dry and heavy, not light and fluffy like most cakes we Americans are used to. The glaze gives it a bit more moisture. Still, I love the nutty and cocoa-laden taste. When mom made it, she usually used walnuts, because we had them falling from the trees in our backyard every fall. Since my wife's tongue gets sores from walnuts, I use hazelnuts. Pecans or english walnuts would also work.

Tools

8-inch dutch oven
6–7 coals below
10–12 coals above

Ingredients

1/2 cups + 1 Tbsp. butter
1/2 cups + 1 Tbsp. sugar
2 eggs

3/4 cups all-purpose flour
1/4 cup cornstarch

3 Tbsp. cocoa

1/2 cup + ground or chopped
 hazelnuts or walnuts
1 cup dark chocolate chips
 (optional)

 Before I start in on the instructions, let me say a few words about the ingredients. First of all, my mom's original recipe used all-purpose flour and cornstarch. I'm told that it's actually a way of conveniently substituting for cake flour, so I think you could try this with 1 full cup of cake flour. Second, the dark chocolate chips were my addition. I like the dark chocolate because it seems to blend well with the flavors of the cocoa and nuts.

 Notice also that there is no leavening in the ingredients. No yeast, no baking soda, or baking powder. That's one of the things that makes it so dense. Still, to make it a bit lighter, it's important to start the ingredients at room temperature and cream the butter and sugar a lot. You want to get as much air into the mixture as possible.

I creamed the butter and sugar using a slotted metal spoon back. It took a long time, and it was a real workout, but eventually it got to the point where it looked like a fluffy frosting. Then, while continuing to beat the mix, I added the eggs in, one at a time.

I took a break and mixed all of the powdered ingredients in another bowl. I sifted the flour to get more aeration. Once that was done, I lit the coals. In this case, I went out and made sure that there were new fresh coals in the chimney since I was cooking other parts of the Christmas dinner. Then I prepared the dutch oven. I oiled and floured the interior and put a disc of parchment in the bottom.

With the dutch oven ready and the coals getting hot, I blended the wet and dry ingredients. It wasn't easy, but I beat them together with as much vigor as I could muster, again, to get as much air as possible into the batter. Finally, I added in the nuts and chocolate chips, mixing everything some more. I poured it into the dutch oven and took the oven out and put it on the coals.

It did take a long time to bake, and it was difficult to tell when it was done since it's a dry mix. Go easy on any replenishment, especially of the bottom coals, because it's easy for the bottom to burn. I Checked it after about 45 minutes, and it was done.

While it was baking, I made the following simple glaze.

Simple Glaze
Ingredients

1/2 cup powdered sugar
hot water or milk to texture

I measured out the powdered sugar into a bowl and added in bits of the hot liquid while stirring it with a small whisk. After a few additions of the liquid, it started to look like a drizzle, and I dusted in a little more sugar to thicken it back up.

When the nusskuchen is done, take it off the coals and let it cool with the lid off. Upend the dutch oven and use your hand to steady the cake out. Slice it and serve it with the glaze. The sweet and bitter flavors combine nicely. I love it!

PUMPKIN CHEESECAKE

For a picture of this recipe, scan this QR code:

I was asked to dutch oven up some dessert for a family barbecue. I'd been wanting to try a cheesecake for some time. After a bit of research, I decided on a pumpkin cheesecake recipe I'd found.

Tools

12–inch dutch oven
10–12 coals below
18–22 coals above

Ingredients

1 pouch graham crackers
2 sticks butter, melted
1/2 bag chocolate chips

4 (8 oz.) pkgs. cream cheese
1 1/2 cups sugar

1 (29 oz.) can pumpkin puree

2 tsp. cinnamon
1 tsp. nutmeg
1 tsp. ginger
1/2 tsp. salt
4 eggs

1/2 bag chocolate chips

I lit some coals and started out making the crust. I ground up the graham crackers in a bowl and mixed in the butter. (I used chocolate graham crackers.) I sprayed the inside of the dutch oven with oil spray and smoothed the crackers across the bottom to form a crust. I sprinkled in half of the bag of chocolate chips.

Then, in a bowl, I combined the cream cheese and the sugar, stirring it up with a big spoon. I tried using a pastry cutter, but it didn't make it easier. Then, I stirred in the can of pumpkin. While I was mixing it in, I added the spices and the eggs.

When I'd mixed everything in as well as I could, I poured it in on top of the crust and topped it off with the rest of the chocolate chips.

Then, I put the oven on the coals. It took a long time to bake, about an hour and 15 minutes, and there are a couple of reasons why. One is that I didn't take into account the time it takes to heat up the dutch oven. So, I was anticipating about a 45 minute cook time, and it took much longer.

CHEESECAKE WITH A TWIST

For a picture of this recipe, scan this QR code:

I wasn't sure what dessert I wanted to make for our Christmas dinner, until my wife suggested that I do a cheesecake.

I figured that since I'd been learning so much about how to do cakes and baking that I'd really like to simplify and just do a good, basic cheesecake without a lot of frills. Then, I could make a couple of different toppings and it would still taste fancy.

As I was doing some research, I found that some of the cheesecakes were done in a water bath in the oven. This was something I'd never heard of before. The basic idea was to put a springform pan, wrapped in aluminum foil to prevent leaking, into a pan full of water, and to put it into the oven. Right away I was intrigued—but also skeptical. Does it make that much of a difference? What's its purpose?

A few more googles turned up some answers. The best reason for doing it is to even the heat distribution around the (relatively delicate) batter. Some said that the steam around the cake also helps prevent cracking on the top.

Well, a dutch oven often suffers from uneven heat, so I thought I'd give it a try. But how? The solution was to do the cake in my 10-inch shallow dutch oven and lower it into a heated water bath in my 14-inch deep oven.

The results were much better than the first time I tried a cheesecake. There were a lot of other things I did differently as well, so I'm not certain it was entirely because of the water bath. But, in the end, it was one of the lightest, fluffiest, creamiest cheesecakes I've ever eaten. It was significantly more work, but the end result was much better.

Tools

10-inch shallow dutch oven
14-inch deep dutch oven
25–28 coals below
16–18 coals above
8-inch dutch oven
10 coals below

Crust
Ingredients

1 1/2 cups graham cracker crumbs
1/4 lb. (1 stick) melted butter
1/4 cup sugar
liberal shakes of ground, dried mint (optional, but it really helps the flavor)

Filling
Ingredients

4 (8 oz.) pkgs. cream cheese, softened
1 1/2 cups sugar
4 eggs
1 Tbsp. cornstarch
1 tsp. vanilla extract
1 Tbsp. lemon juice
1 cup heavy whipping cream

Topping
Ingredients

1 1/2 cups frozen fruit (strawberries)
1/2 cup sugar
shakes of cinnamon and nutmeg
water as needed

126   MARK HANSEN

I started out by taking the ingredients out of the fridge so they could get up to room temperature. Then, as usual, I got a lot of coals ready. I used a lot on the ovens, and it was a fairly long cooking time, so I needed a side fire handy as well to keep replenishing the coals.

Before making any of the ingredients, I set the 10-inch inside the 14-inch and filled it with water until it came a bit up the side of the 10-inch. That was a lot of water, and it takes a while to get it heated up. I took the 10-inch out and put the 14-inch on and under the coals, with the lid on. I wanted the water oven to be as preheated as possible, maybe even simmering.

Then, I made the crust. I actually didn't have any graham crackers, so I ended up using honey-flavored oat breakfast cereal O's. It still tasted fine. I mixed in the melted butter, the sugar, and the mint and pressed the mixture into place at the bottom of the dutch oven. There was some debate as to whether you were supposed to mold it up the sides or not. Since I was serving it straight from the dutch, I didn't fuss with it and just made it level.

Then, I got a big mixing bowl and creamed the cream cheese and the sugar together. I have this potato masher with kinda small holes, and it worked perfectly. I did it a lot, trying to incorporate a lot of air into the mix. It's not as easy to do cream cheese as it is to do butter, so it was a tough job.

Then, I added the eggs, one at a time, creaming each one into the mix as I went. After that, I added the other ingredients and mixed more and more. I've got a pretty stiff whisk, which I used to finish it up.

By this time, the water was bubbly hot, so I poured the batter into the 10-inch dutch oven, shook it a bit to settle it in, and put it into the 14-inch. I kept the 10-inch lid off, but closed the lid of the 14-inch. I replenished the coals and went on cooking the rest of the dinner.

I kept a close eye on it. I didn't lift the lid much, probably about every half hour or so. I ended up cooking it just under an hour and a half. It had puffed up pretty high in the 10-inch at that point. It even cracked a little on the top because it had swelled so much. Maybe the steam doesn't help it in that way much!

I pulled it out and set it aside to cool. Another thing my research told me was to let it cool slowly. It settled back down in the dutch oven as it did. Finally, when it was cool, I put it outside with the lid on to chill.

In my 8-inch dutch oven, with about 10 coals underneath, I mixed the topping ingredients. I let it come up to temperature and simmer to reduce into a syrup. Once it was done, I let it cool. My dear wife also made a chocolate drizzle.

It was delicious and rich. I recommend cutting thin slices!

DUTCH OVEN RICE PUDDING
WITH APPLE CAVIAR

(An Experiment in Molecular Gastronomy Spherification)

For a picture of this recipe, scan this QR code:

A long time ago, back when John at mormonfoodie.com first encouraged me to start Mark's Black Pot, there was a movement forming among foodies called *molecular gastronomy*. It was kinda weird, kinda exciting, and kinda new. It involved using science—particularly chemistry—to make some new and unusual sort of taste experiences.

Recently, my son encountered some examples on YouTube, and we started looking into being able to do it ourselves. It's both simple and complex, so it took a bit of research. One of the simplest processes is one called basic spherification. Here's how it goes.

1. Pick a juice or puree.
2. Mix it with one chemical, a kind of salt.
3. Drizzle drops of it into a bath of water with another chemical, a different kind of salt.
4. The chemicals instantly react to form a coating, a membrane, around the sphere of juice.
5. Rinse it off and serve it, and it looks like juice caviar. When you put it in your mouth, it pops with the flavor of the juice.

So, we got a kit of the chemicals and gave it a try. Actually, it took two tries. So, I'm going to share the process here, because it was a lot of fun, and we learned a lot doing it.

But first, a bit of tradition to go with our modernist dessert.

I wanted to make something to go with it. I mean, you don't just eat caviar straight from the bottle, do you? I started thinking about things to put it on, a proverbial canvas to carry the paint. I wanted the base flavors to be subtle, not strong, but complementary to the caviar's own. I decided on a rice pudding and an apple juice caviar.

So, this recipe is not so much about molecular gastronomy as it is the prep for it. Then, in the next one, I'll tell you how to do the caviar.

Dutch Oven Rice Pudding

Tools

8-inch dutch oven
12–13 coals below

Ingredients

3/4 cup uncooked white rice
1 1/2 cups water

1 1/2 cups milk
1/3 cup white sugar
1/4 tsp. salt

1 egg, beaten

1/2 cup milk

2/3 cup golden raisins
1 Tbsp. butter
1/2 tsp. vanilla extract
cinnamon
nutmeg

First of all, I got some coals going, and I cooked the rice. Over time, I've developed a way to do rice that works for me almost every time, without burning. I put one part rice and two parts water into either my 8-inch or 10-inch dutch oven and set it on coals to boil. I watch closely to notice when the steam starts venting out from under the lid. At that point, it's been boiling for several minutes already. I mark that time and let it boil for an additional 10 minutes. Then, I pull it off the coals and let it sit for another 15–20 minutes. At no time in this process do I lift the lid! Only after it's all done.

In this case, however, instead of bringing it in and serving it, I put it back on the coals and stirred in the milk, sugar, and salt. I put the lid back on and let it come back up to a simmer and cooked it for another 15–20 minutes.

I whisked the milk and the egg together. I decided to temper the egg to keep it from cooking and congealing when it suddenly hit the hot rice and milk. I put the egg and milk mixture in a bowl next to the dutch oven, and, while whisking the egg mixture, I gradually added big spoonfuls of hot rice and milk. The idea is to gradually bring the temperature of the egg up so that it blends in without scrambling the egg. When it was all hot, I poured it into the dutch oven. I added the final flavorings and let it cook for another 4–5 minutes.

A note about the seasonings: go easy. The idea is to create a platform for the apple juice caviar, so you want a little flavor but not too much. Of course, if you are making the pudding just for a dessert and are not putting anything on top of it, then season it all you want!

Finally, I let it cool. Actually, because our first attempt at spherification bombed, I ended up refrigerating the pudding and bringing it out the next day. It was delicious, even the next day!

MOLECULAR GASTRONOMY

So, once again, we're talking about molecular gastronomy, or, as it's sometimes called, modernist cooking. When I hear that term, I wonder what will come next, maybe post-modernist cooking? Will we be debating the existence of food?

But I digress . . .

As I said last time, the first attempt my son and I made at basic spherification failed miserably, and we chalked it up to a learning experience. We made some adjustments the second time and it turned out really good. I'm sure that as we do it more and more, we'll get better and better and understand it well.

As you go through the ingredients, you'll notice that the amounts are in grams, not in cups or tablespoons. That's because this is chemistry, and chemists don't measure in teaspoons. Accurate measurements are very important in this process.

Here's what you need.

Tools

pH test strips
a scale that measures with an
   accuracy of 0.1 grams
small cups for measuring and
   dispensing the chemicals
a blender or a whisk
4 clean bowls, preferably clear glass
a large plastic medical syringe
a small strainer or spoon with small
   holes

Ingredients

at least 1000 grams apple juice
5 grams sodium citrate
5 grams sodium alginate
about a liter of clean water
5 grams calcium chloride

I started out with a lot of apple juice, and to intensify the flavor, I boiled it and reduced it down to about half. To do the spherification, you'll need exactly 500 grams, so I started with more than double that. Confession: I did this step in a saucepan on my stove. I know I should have done it on coals in my dutch oven. I hang my head in shame.

Then, I let it cool in the fridge. When it was at about room temperature, I pulled it out and tested the pH with the test strips. There were two possible reasons why the first one failed. One was that the juice might have been too acidic. The best results happen when your pH is more than 3.6. The first batch tested at 4, so it should have been okay, but it was really close. Also, many fruit juices have added calcium, which can begin the spherification reaction too soon. In either case, sodium citrate is the answer. So, the second time, I added some to the juice. I'd read that this measurement is not as critical.

Once that was dissolved, it was time to make the sphere base solution. I measured exactly 500 grams of the reduced juice. For the spherification to work, you must have accurate measurements. My scale wasn't so accurate, and that also caused problems the first time. I was much more careful, but I think I got lucky the second time. I also measured out 5 grams of the sodium alginate.

I got the blender out. (The instructions say you can use a whisk, but I was a bit nervous, so I used the blender.) While blending the juice, I gradually tipped in the sodium alginate. The first time, it got very thick. I think we had added too much, and I think it also reacted with the juice. The second time, it did get a little thicker, but it was still very runny.

Even though the sodium alginate looks dissolved, it needs some time to fully hydrate and to be fully absorbed into the juice. Also, the air bubbles have to dissipate. I set it in the fridge for an hour or longer.

After a time in the fridge, the liquid looked clear, but there were still some bubbles on top. I scooped these away with a spoon.

While I let the sphere base solution get a bit warmer, I made the setting bath. I set up three bowls. In the first, I put 500 grams of water. I used tap water, but the instructions also recommend using distilled water. I think next time, I'll do that. While whisking, I gradually added the calcium chloride and stirred it until it was fully dissolved. I filled each of the other bowls about 3/4 of the way with water.

I bought a molecular gastronomy chemical kit to do this, and it came with a big plastic syringe; however, I have a son with special health care needs, so we have these things all over the house. I sucked up the sphere base solution into the syringe and, from a height of about 2–3 inches, dribbled it into the setting bath. It's important to not press too fast, because you'll get a worm, not a sphere. I like having a clear glass bowl, because it was easier to see the resulting caviar spheres from the side of the bowl than it was from above. The fact that the apple juice was a light color didn't help much either.

Once I'd squeezed out about a full syringe of juice, I gently stirred up the water to see what we had. I stirred over the spheres rather than through them and let the water motion move them around. I let them set in the bath for about a minute or two, and then lifted them out with the strainer. I poured them immediately into the first water bath, rinsed them, and then into the second water bath.

I got a small bowl and put a heaping spoonful of rice pudding into the center. I placed the apple caviar beads around and on top of it. It was an elegant presentation, and the flavor was wonderful. It was fun to try and a great learning experience!

By the way, the spheres keep gelling, even though they've been rinsed off, so it's important to serve them as quickly as possible. A great video instruction series can be found at http://chefsteps.com/mp.

CHAPTER 8

BREADS

AS I WAS FIRST LEARNING HOW TO COOK in a dutch oven, I found breads to be particularly challenging. Sometimes my loaves or rolls would turn out beautifully light and delicious, and sometimes they would turn out like a brick, usable only as a doorstop or a curling rock. Baking a good loaf of bread can be a bit challenging in the best of conditions. When you're baking outdoors in a dutch oven, many of the constants, like heat and time, become variables. It was common for one of those variables to jump out and surprise me. I was, however, undaunted and did a lot of research reading and practice baking. Finally, after several years, I got to the point where I could confidently turn out a consistently well-made, well-baked loaf.

In the process, I wrote a book called *Dutch Oven Breads*, which is specifically about the process of making bread in a dutch oven. It was also published by Cedar Fort under the Hobble Creek imprint. My goal was to explain it all in such a way that you wouldn't have to spend three years practicing to get good results.

So, here are some things to keep in mind that will help you bake better loaves of bread!

1. Buy and Read *Dutch Oven Breads*

I know this is kinda obvious. Forgive me for the shameless plug. *Dutch Oven Breads* really does cover a lot of detailed knowledge that's beyond the scope of this book.

To get the book, scan this QR code:

2. Use Fresh Bread Flour

Bread flour has a higher protein content than all-purpose flour does, and those proteins combine more quickly to form gluten strands, which trap the gasses the yeast germs are burpin' out. You can use all-purpose flour, but you'll be kneading it for a lot longer.

Also, use fresh flour. After a while, the oils in the flour oxidize, and they don't allow the gluten strands to form as well, even in as little as a month. Buy smaller packages of bread flour more frequently and use them quickly.

3. Knead to the Windowpane Test

A big problem I had was knowing how long to knead the dough. Rather than use some arbitrary measure, like a clock, use the windowpane test.

After kneading a while, cut off and roll up a ball about the size of a ping-pong ball. Flatten it in your palm, and with your fingers begin to turn it and stretch it. If you can pull it to the point where it becomes translucent, allowing light to shine through, without tearing, then you know that the gluten has developed and it's ready to rise. If it tears, fold the dough ball back in and keep kneading.

By the way, I like to knead by hand, adding bits of flour along the way if needed, to adjust the amount of wetness and pliability.

4. Preheat the Dutch Oven, or at Least the Lid

Most dutch oven bread recipes I'd read said to put the coals on and let the bread bake, but much of the early heat in that process goes to gradually warming up the dutch oven. If a loaf of bread is exposed to a sudden rush of heat, the air bubbles will swiftly expand, causing the bread to spring and get more fluffy.

5. Bake to Temperature, Not to Color

I had a lot of troubles knowing when it was done. Sometimes, I would overestimate the heat, either on the top or the bottom, and it would look deliciously brown on top but still be doughy in the middle. For light, white breads, cook until the center measures 190–200 degrees. For darker breads, like ryes and whole wheats, cook until it measures 185–190 degrees.

6. Cool Completely

When it's at the right temperature, invert the dutch oven and toss the loaf out onto a cooling rack and let it sit and cool. This is *very* difficult, because it will look and smell so inviting. But, it's *still cooking*. It's not done yet. Only once it has cooled to near ambient temperature is the cooking complete.

These five tips will help you bake better bread loaves. The recipes below are great, too!

JODI'S SANDWICH BREAD

For a picture of this recipe, scan this QR code:

As I mentioned in the article above, I tried many times to make various loaves. Here is an entry from the marksblackpot.com blog which will show this learning process.

"So, even though I've done this bread before, I'm writing about it again, because I learned something very important. In the process, I've salvaged my bread-baking confidence. Let me tell you the story.

"Over the last few months, I've tried to make some breads, but they've not worked out well. I first noticed it when I tried to make my sister's whole wheat recipe. It was very difficult to knead it enough to get a good gluten windowpane [see page 133] going on. After 30–40 minutes or so, it would kinda come together, but not really, and I would give up. It would rise, but not as I hoped it would, and when it all baked, it was heavy with a hard crust.

"I just figured that it was because that's how whole wheat is, right? But that's not how it was when Mom made it many years ago.

"Then my wife tried to make rolls that ended up like bricks. I thought to myself, *She didn't knead them enough*. Fortunately, I didn't say anything, because when I made white bread a few days later, I had the same problem.

"I was really down about it. Here I'd been all confident that I was really learning how to make bread, and suddenly nothing was working! I just didn't get it at all!

"Gradually it dawned on me that the white flour I'd been using might be bad. It had been a part of Jodi's step-dad's food storage for years, and he had given it to us. I checked with my sister, who's been a wonderful source of inspiration and guidance, and she thought it might be the problem too.

"So, when I did the bread for the Christmas feast, I bought a fresh batch of bread flour and did it all again, just like I had before. Right away, I could tell a difference. The dough was more white where the bad dough had been kind of yellow. It felt better in my fingers as I kneaded it. This was how I remembered it. I got to the point where I could do a full gluten windowpane in about 10 minutes of kneading.

"This recipe is from my wife's mom and has been a family tradition for years. I feel pretty good that I can pull it off regularly now. It's my go-to bread recipe.

Tools

12-inch dutch oven
17–18 coals above, 10–12 below for
    350°F (Use more coals in cold
    weather.)

Ingredients

1 cup hot water
1 Tbsp. yeast
3/4 cup honey

4–5 cups flour, with probably about one
    cup to be added during kneading

a pinch of salt
1 cups milk (mixed from powder)
1 egg
2 Tbsp. oil
an egg to coat the top

"First, I activated the yeast. I got fully hot tap water and added the honey to it. This cooled it significantly, but it was still quite warm. I added the yeast to it and let it sit and grow foamy for a while.

"In a separate bowl, I added the flour and the other ingredients. I added in the yeast/honey mix and stirred it all up with a wooden spoon. It came loose from the sides of the bowl but was still quite sticky.

"I floured the countertop and dumped out the dough. I sprinkled more flour onto the dough ball and started kneading. It was still sticky, but I kept kneading and gradually sprinkling on more flour until it no longer stuck to my fingers and the table.

"I kept kneading until I could make a good windowpane. For those who don't understand that yet, cut off a chunk of the dough and make a ball about the size of a golf ball. Then you stretch it out with your fingers like you're making a pizza. Stretch it until it tears. If you can stretch it thin and translucent without it tearing, then you've achieved the 'gluten windowpane,' and you're done kneading. If it keeps tearing, you must knead it more.

"Once it was ready, I used spray oil on the mixing bowl and put it back in. I sprayed another coating of oil on top to keep it from drying out. I covered it with a towel and set it aside to rise.

"It rose up nicely, just like I had hoped it would. That was the second sign that it was working.

"Once it had risen, I went outside and started up the coals. It would take a while for the coals and the oven to get ready while I proofed the bread.

"I came back in and dumped out the dough. Using one of those cool pastry cutters, I cut it into quarters and formed each quarter into a ball. You pull the surface around and underneath and pinch it together. That stretches the surface smooth. I quickly sprayed oil into the dutch oven and put each dough ball on the bottom, like in quarters. Then I set the dutch oven aside to rise again (which is called *proofing*).

"In the meantime, I took the dutch oven lid outside and poured some coals onto it, about 20 or so to preheat it. After about 20 minutes, the dough balls had risen some, and I knew the lid was good and hot. I coated the dough balls with the beaten egg. Then, outside, I made a ring of coals and set the dutch oven onto it and closed on the lid.

"I let it cook for about 35–45 minutes. Every 15 minutes or so, I rotated the lid about a quarter turn and lifted and turned the oven itself. This helps reposition the coals relative to the oven and the bread inside so you don't get hot spots. After about a half hour, I put a cooking thermometer into the dough and reclosed the lid. That allows me to check the internal temperature of the bread. Soft breads like this are done at about 180–200 degrees.

"When it was done, I pulled the oven off the coals. I let the bread cool a little in the oven with the lid off. (I need to get one of those drying racks so that the bottom can air out while it cools. Then the bottom won't be so moist and squishy!)

"So, the lesson I learned is that if you're using food storage flour, make sure you actually use it and not just keep it under your stairs for a hundred years. If it's so old that it doesn't respond, throw it out. There's not much use for it. My wife even tried to make brownies with it using baking powder, but it didn't even work well for that."

For a video of this recipe, scan this QR code:

SOFT DINNER ROLLS

For a picture of this recipe, scan this QR code:

I was making dinner one day, and Jodi mentioned that she wanted dinner rolls. My mind immediately jumped to a certain buffet restaurant we go to. Their rolls are light and fluffy, almost to the point of having no substance. Generally, I like my bread with a little body (sometimes a lot), but then I also like learning how to get the results I want. So, I thought I'd take on the challenge. The results that day were good, and very light.

Tools

10-inch dutch oven
12 coals below
20–22 coals above

Ingredients

2 tsp. yeast (or 1 pkg.)
1/4 cup warm water (105°F–110°F)
1/2 Tbsp. sugar

1 cup milk, just to scalding hot
   (do not simmer or boil)

1/4 cup melted butter

4 cups bread flour
1 tsp. salt
1 egg, lightly beaten
2 Tbsp. butter, melted, for brushing

The process for these rolls is similar to my standard process for bread, with a few changes. I start out by activating the yeast in a bowl with the warm water and the sugar. I set that aside to get frothy for about 10 minutes or so.

Then, I heat up the milk and the butter. If I'd been out in the wild, I could've done this in a dutch oven, like my 8-inch oven, over about 12 coals, but since I was in a bit of a hurry, I did it in the microwave. May the gods of cast iron forgive me!

I sifted the bread flour into a mixing bowl and added the salt and egg. I stirred in the yeast mix and the milk mix. It was pretty sticky. When I turned it out on the table and started kneading, I didn't add much flour on the table. I wanted it to be a wet dough to make it lighter. (Not as wet as the no-knead or a ciabatta/focaccia dough, but definitely more loose than a regular sandwich bread.) I kneaded it to a good windowpane. Then I oiled the bowl, put the dough in it, covered it, and set it aside to rise.

I let it rise a bit higher than normal, in both the first and second fermentations.

After the first rise, I cut it into eighths and rolled each piece into a small ball. I put these into the base of my oiled 10-inch dutch oven. I set the oven aside for the rolls to rise while I lit up some coals. Once the coals were ready, I put about 20–25 of them on the lid of the dutch oven to preheat it. After about 15–20 minutes of heating, the rolls had risen well. I set up the coals as listed above and started the baking.

After about 15 minutes, I turned the lid and the oven and put the thermometer in the dough. They had sprung up nicely and were just starting to brown. About 10 minutes later, the thermometer read about 190 degrees, and they were ready to come off the coals. I didn't go all the way to 200 degrees, because I wanted the rolls to be softer.

I brought them in, turned them out of the dutch oven, and set them on a cooling rack. While they were still hot, I coated the top with butter, which immediately melted onto the crust. They cooled while I cooked the rest of the dinner.

As I said before, they were lighter than most loaves I'd done. I think that making the dough wetter helped, as well as the extra rise time.

BAKING BREAD FOR CHURCH

Spoiler alert! I'm going to get personal in this recipe. I'm going to talk about my church and my faith.

But—I hope it won't be in a preachy way. I hope it relates to the core of why we make food and how we make some of the food and ingredient choices we make for one circumstance or another. It really goes to the heart of the art of cooking. This was the first chance I'd had to take an emotion and express it through ingredients, process, and, finally, the end result.

If you don't want to be bothered with all that, I won't be offended. You can skip down below and read what I hope will be a good, solid, yummy bread recipe. On the other hand, I hope you'll also take a moment and think about a time when you've cooked something expressive.

Okay, here we go . . .

One Sunday, I had the opportunity to provide the bread for our ward's sacrament service. For those not of my faith, let me take a moment to explain it. In a Mormon chapel, every Sunday, one of the meetings (the most important one theologically) is sacrament meeting. We listen to talks (that we call sermons), and sing, of course, but it's the actual ordinance of the sacrament that's the key portion of the meeting. In it, baptized members of the Church eat a tiny piece of bread and drink a tiny cup of water in symbolic remembrance of the Savior's suffering and Atonement for us. It's a big deal to us (or at least it should be). It's a part of our weekly renewal and repentance.

So, I got the chance to provide the bread for this service last week. Now, normally, the bread is just store-bought, sliced bread. It doesn't matter, theologically or doctrinally, what bread you use. In the Last Supper, Jesus himself probably used some variant on a pita or an unleavened flat bread.

Since I love to bake bread in the dutch oven, I got up early in the morning to bake the loaves that would be used in our sacrament service.

Part of the reason I bring this up is to share my thought processes as I decided what I was going to do. My first thought was to pull out all the stops and make an amazing herb loaf, or the cocoa bread, or maybe even rye. Practical reasons stopped the rye since it would take too long to rise. And the others didn't seem right. I wanted to give it my best. I mean, this is for church, right? In some ways, I'm baking for God here!

Then I thought about the service itself, and I realized that if I did one of those wonderful breads, then lots of people would be tasting it and thinking, "Wow, that bread is really great!" And suddenly, they're pulled out of the ordinance. They're thinking about the bread, not the Atonement.

The bread would have to be simple and plain. It would have to be the best simple and plain bread I'd ever baked. In that sense, it might even be a bit zen-like, or like a Shaker hymn.

Anyway, I got out my recipes and identified a pure and simple bread recipe. I did add a little olive oil, and maybe an egg for a touch of richness, and the dough turned out to be a very damp, rustic dough, which, I think, added to the fluffy lightness in the end. I also doubled what's below and baked two loaves, one for my family. As I gathered up the ingredients, I said a quick prayer and started in.

Tools

12-inch dutch oven
14–15 coals below
18–22 coals above

Ingredients

1 Tbsp. yeast
2 cups water (110°F)
2 Tbsp. sugar

1 tsp. salt
2 Tbsp. olive oil
1 egg (optional)

4 cups fresh bread flour, adding as
   much as 1 cup more during kneading

I started by getting some warm tap water. (To touch, it feels like a nice, hot shower, even just a little too hot.) I added the yeast, the sugar, and stirred it up. I set that aside to activate.

Meanwhile, I sifted the flour into a large mixing bowl and added the salt. Once the yeast was nice and frothy, I added that and the oil into the mix and stirred it all up.

I scooped it out onto a well-floured countertop and started kneading, shaking on more flour as needed. As I mentioned, when it passed the windowpane test, it was still a damp, loose dough, but, obviously, not as sticky as when I started. I shaped it into a large ball and set it in the oiled bowl to rise, covered with a tea towel.

The recipe has a lot of yeast in it, so it rose fairly quickly. When it was more than doubled, I punched it down, reshaped it, and set it in a cloth-lined basket for the second rising. As I reshaped it, I pinched a seam along the bottom and put the pinched seam side up in the basket. That way, when I dumped it out into the hot dutch oven, the seam would be on the bottom of the loaf.

I lit up some coals, and when they were getting white, I set up the proper coals over and under a 12-inch dutch oven. I had lightly oiled the interior of the oven, and I let it preheat, empty, with the lid on, for about 15–20 minutes.

Finally, it was all ready to bake. I opened up the dutch oven and turned the dough ball in from the basket. I sliced the top and put the cover back on. After about 15 minutes, I opened up the lid and put in a short-stemmed thermometer and rotated the lid and the dutch oven. It was a pretty breezy day, so I added 2–3 coals to the bottom and 3–4 to the top. After another 20 minutes, it was done (to an internal temperature of 190–200 degrees). I brought it in and turned it out onto a cooling rack.

After it cooled, right before we left to take it to church, I sliced it up, and it was probably the lightest, fluffiest loaf I'd ever baked. I tasted a corner, and it was just what I wanted: pure, simple, and perfectly cooked.

At church, my oldest son got to participate in the service, as he often does. It was very special to me to hear him say the prayer to bless the bread and to watch it being passed to the congregation. As it was passed to me, I felt a peace and happiness that I think comes from being able to give something—an offering— and know it was accepted.

ITALIAN BREAD

This bread is called an *indirect* bread by some, because it has a preferment (called a *biga*) before the actual main mixing and main rise. In this case, I chose to do it overnight. We also ended up shaping this dough into balls and hollowing them out to use as bread bowls for split-pea soup.

Biga
Ingredients

2 1/2 cups unbleached bread flour
1/2 tsp. yeast
3/4 cup to 1 cup water at room temperature.

I mixed the ingredients above in a bowl, turned them out onto a floured tabletop, and kneaded them for a few minutes until they all came together. At this stage, I didn't worry too much about the dough forming a windowpane. I just wanted it smooth, like a bread dough in and of itself. Then I oiled it and put it under plastic wrap in a bowl. I put it in the fridge overnight.

If it hadn't been so late at night when I made the Biga, I would have just set it out to rise for a couple of hours and then put it in the fridge.

The next morning, I took it out of the fridge and set it out to come back up to room temperature. At that point, I chopped it up into about 10 pieces. I gathered the ingredients for the main dough mix.

Main Dough
Ingredients

3 1/2 cups of biga (pretty much all of what I mixed the night before)
2 1/2 cups unbleached bread flour
1 2/3 tsp. salt
1 Tbsp. sugar
1 tsp. yeast
1 Tbsp. olive oil
3/4 cup water, about 100°F

I mixed all of the ingredients in a bowl, dumped the dough out onto a floured countertop, and kneaded it for real. I kneaded it for almost 20 minutes, and at that point, I got a good windowpane. I set it aside to rise on the countertop.

This time, it rose quite well. After only about two hours, it was ready to shape. Before I degassed it and began working it, however, I got some coals lit. Then I came in and shaped the dough into four equal quarters and made them into boule shapes (balls). I put these in a square configuration on a piece of parchment on a plate.

Soon the coals were hot, and I put an oiled dutch oven on and under a lot of coals, probably a total of about 30, with an oven thermometer inside. After about 30–40, it read 375 degrees. I would actually recommend going even higher, but then you'll have to replenish your coals. The dough had proofed up nicely. I lifted the dough balls up by the parchment paper and lowered them into the dutch oven. I closed the lid and marked the time.

After about 15 minutes, I rotated the oven and the lid so that it was positioned differently in relation to the coals (to prevent hot spots on the oven). I also peeked in and inserted a thermometer into the now-baking bread.

After about another 20 minutes, the thermometer read 200 degrees, and I knew it was done. I pulled it off the coals and dropped the bread onto my cooling racks.

It was at this point that I told my son I was going to cook the pea soup, and he suggested using the bread as bowls. They were the perfect size and shape. It was brilliant!

For your reference and convenience, here's the soup recipe. (This recipe is also found on page 72 of the Specialty Main Dishes chapter.)

DUTCH OVEN SPLIT-PEA SOUP WITH HAM

Tools

12-inch dutch oven
15–20 coals below

Ingredients

1 sliced onion
4–5 cloves of garlic, minced
2 stalks chopped celery
6 cups water, at least half of which could be chicken stock
1 lb. bag of dried split peas

1 ham bone with lots of meat left on it.
1 diced potato
generous shakes of oregano, parsley, and chili powder
salt and coarse ground pepper to taste

First, I light up some coals and let them start getting white. I put about a tablespoon of olive oil in the bottom of my dutch oven and heat it up. I chop up the veggies while it's all getting going.

Once the oil is hot, I drop in the onion, garlic, and celery to sauté. Remember, if it's hot enough, they'll sizzle as soon as you drop them in. I stir them together and salt them a little.

Once the garlic is brown and the onions are translucent, I pour in the liquid. I use a bullion powder to make it all chicken stock. Sometimes, if I have any, I use my own homemade stock.

Then I add all the other ingredients except the herbs and chili powder and bring the soup back up to a boil.

Once it's simmering, I add in the herbs and the chili powder. I add the chili powder a bit at a time. I shake in some, let it simmer for 15 minutes or so, and then taste it. I add some more, wait, and taste it. I want it to have an edge, but I don't want it to have a recognizable chili taste. Season with salt and pepper to taste, but be cautious, because the ham is already salty.

DUTCH OVEN PIZZA IN THE RAIN!

For a picture of this recipe, scan this QR code:

Normally, I cook on Sundays. But on Fridays, I come home from work early. On this particular Friday, I was kinda hankering to cook something on the back porch in the dutch ovens. As I drove home, I was a little deterred by the drops of rain on my windshield and the *wikk, wikk, wikk* of my wipers. But I decided to go for it anyway.

I didn't want to do anything complex or fancy this time. I decided on pizza. It had been a long time since I'd last done that. In fact, as I recall, it was another rainy day in March of the previous year or so when I last did it. Jodi's not a big fan of pizza, so whenever I suggest it, she comes up with other ideas. But she was working late that night.

So, I stopped off and bought some supplies—pepperoni, canadian bacon, mozzarella, and olives.

The first thing I did, of course, was to mix up the crust so it could rise.

The secret to good pizza is pretty easy. The wrong way to do it is known as *GIGO*.

Those of you who are into computers, especially programming, already understand this term. For the rest of us in the real world, GIGO means "garbage in, garbage out." If you make a dish with garbage, it's going to taste like garbage. The opposite is also true. If you use good stuff to make your food, it will taste great. So, to make good pizza, don't scrimp on your ingredients. A good dough recipe, good sauce, and good toppings make a great pizza.

Tools

Two 12-inch dutch ovens
8 coals below
16 coals above
(In this case, because of the rain, I did the coals differently.)

Crust
Ingredients

1 1/2 cups warm water
1 Tbsp. yeast
1 Tbsp. sugar
1/4 tsp. salt
3 Tbsp. olive oil
4 cups flour

I started by putting the yeast in some of the warm water to let it foam up. My experience has shown me that things tend to rise slowly or poorly in my house (which could be the altitude), so I add a little extra yeast.

Mix the other ingredients in a bowl, add the water and the yeast, and knead it into a ball. I also put in a little extra sugar to help the extra yeast along. Use the last bit of flour to adjust the smoothness of the dough—not too dry, not too sticky. You might not use exactly 4 cups. I sprayed the bowl with cooking spray, put the dough ball in it, and then sprayed the top of the dough.

I set it aside to rise.

After a half hour to 45 minutes, I went outside and lit up 50 coals or so. Once the coals were glowing, I scattered them into two groups and put two 12-inch dutch ovens on them. I split a pound of mild italian sausage between the two ovens, and let that start to brown.

In the meantime, I mixed up the sauce.

Sauce
Ingredients

1 small can tomato sauce
1 small can tomato paste
1 Tbsp. black pepper
1 Tbsp. celery salt
1 Tbsp. oregano (maybe a little more)

Actually, those amounts on the spices are estimates. Just go until it smells rich!

My timing was good. Just about the time that the sausage was browned, the dough had risen enough. I brought the dutch ovens inside and pulled the sausage out. In the bottom of each oven, now well greased from the sausage, I added some minced garlic (about a tablespoon), a bit of butter (about a tablespoon), and some generous shakings of celery salt.

I took the now-risen ball of dough, split it in half, and formed one half into the pizza flat. I put it into the bottom of one dutch oven. The other half of the dough was placed in the other dutch oven.

Onto that went the sauce and a thin layer of cheeses. I bought one of those shredded italian cheese blends, with mozzarella, provolone, parmesan, and romano. Mmmmm. . . .

Then, I piled on the toppings—the sausage; canadian bacon; pepperoni; fresh, sliced onions; and olives! And finally, the entire thing was buried in a thick blanket of cheese. I was doing this all as fast as I could since the coals were outside getting rained on.

So, I took the ovens back outside. I put about 12 coals in a circle and put one of the ovens on top of them. Then I put about 14 coals on top of that oven. I stacked the second oven on top of the first one and put about 14 coals on top of the second oven.

After about 15 minutes, I unstacked them, turned them, and restacked them to distribute the heat more evenly. Finally, after about 35 minutes, it was done!

Dang yummy pizza, and very filling! Any leftovers make wonderful lunches!

SANDWICH BUNS

Author's note: a recipe for Pulled Chicken Sandwiches is in the section on chicken (page 31), which goes really well with these sandwich buns.

Tools

12-inch shallow dutch oven
12–14 coals below
24–26 coals above

Topping
Ingredients

1 egg
sesame seeds
poppy seeds

Ingredients

1/2 cup of 110°F water
2 Tbsp. active dry yeast
3/4 cup of 110°F milk
1/4 cup sugar
3 Tbsp. butter
2 tsp. salt
4–5 cups fresh bread flour (If the flour is old, add 1 Tbsp. vital wheat gluten.)
1 egg

I started out by activating the yeast in the water. I set it aside to get all foamy while I gathered the rest of the ingredients. I always use bread yeast when making yeast breads, but if it gets more than a couple of months old, I add a little bit of vital wheat gluten powder. Otherwise, it will never get decent gluten development and won't rise well.

I added all the dry ingredients together (using just 4 cups of flour), poured in the wet ingredients, and mixed them all into a dough ball. I turned the dough out onto my floured tabletop and began kneading. I added more flour as needed to make it the right texture and not so sticky. Finally, after 10 minutes or so, it passed the windowpane test. I placed it in an oiled bowl and set it aside to rise.

After it rose, I lit some coals. I punched down the dough and cut it into 8 equal parts. These I shaped into dough balls. I flattened them under my palm on the tabletop. All of these went into the oiled dutch oven. I took the dutch oven lid out and poured a lot of burning coals on top of it to preheat it.

After about 20–25 minutes, the dough balls were rising again and the lid was hot. I whipped up an egg and coated the top of each bun using a basting brush and sprinkled on the other toppings. Then I put on the lid and adjusted the coals above and below. I baked them for about 30–35 minutes, or until the internal temperature hit about 180–200 degrees.

When they were done, I pulled them out and put them on a cooling rack. Once they were cooled, it was easy to slice them horizontally and serve them with the Barbecue Pulled Chicken, a burger, or whatever else I wanted between the delicious halves of these buns!

CORNBREAD

For a picture of this recipe, scan this QR code:

Awhile back, some old family friends invited us to a family chili cook-off. Of course, I obliged, and I made some of my delicious chilli (see page 8).

I also made some cornbread. My favorite way of making cornbread in the past was to whip up a cornbread mix, then a yellow cake mix, and then stir the two together. I thought there would be a way to make both of these from scratch, so I did some research and came up with this recipe. It ended up more like a cake with a bit of corn flavor, but it was nice and moist and not so crumbly as typical cornbread. When I prepared this recipe for the blog, I added a bit more cornmeal to it.

Tools

10-inch dutch oven
9–10 coals below
18–20 coals above

Ingredients

1/4 cup softened butter (the softer the better)
1 cup white sugar
3 eggs

1 cup cornmeal
2 1/4 cups flour
1 1/2 Tbsp. baking powder

1 tsp. salt
light shakes of cinnamon and nutmeg

1/2 cup vegetable oil
1 Tbsp. honey
1 3/4 cups whole milk

I started by lighting the coals. (Once they are white-edged, a lot of them will go on the dutch oven lid to preheat it.)

The first step is to cream the butter and sugar together. I used the back of a big serving spoon to whip the two together and incorporate as much air as possible. Do this for several minutes until it's nice and fluffy.

I added in the eggs, one at a time, beating and blending as I went.

By this time, my arm was tired, and I took a break. I mixed the dry ingredients together into one bowl, and the remaining wet ingredients into another. After all this, I went out and put the coals on the lid.

I added half of the dry ingredients and continued mixing. Then I added half of the wet and mixed some more. While still mixing, I added the remainder of each. At that point, it turned into a nice batter, which I finished up with a wire whisk to break apart the dry clumps.

I cut a circle of parchment paper to line the bottom, even though I planned on serving cut squares directly from the dutch so I wouldn't need to flip it out like a cake. Still, I went with it. I sprayed the sides of the dutch oven with oil as well.

I poured in the batter and took the dutch oven out and set it under the heated lid. I counted out the proper coals above and below and set it to bake. I rotated the dutch oven after about 15 minutes, and after about 35 minutes, it was done! I brought it in and let it cool.

It was delicious, and it served up well next to everyone's chili.

CHAPTER 9

GENERAL DUTCH OVEN INFORMATION

THANKS SO MUCH FOR BUYING and (I'm hoping) enjoying this book. I've sure enjoyed cooking these recipes and blogging them over the years.

This final chapter is a compilation of a lot of good, basic information about dutch ovening. It has answers to things like, "How do I shop for a dutch oven and what else do I need?" "How many coals should I use?" "What if my dutch oven gets rusty?" Also, there are a couple of fun articles about how to use chili peppers and the recipes for some fun flavored oils I've made.

SHOPPING FOR A DUTCH OVEN

A lot of people ask me what to look for when they're shopping to buy a dutch oven.

I guess the real title for this section should be "How to shop for a dutch oven and buy one that's best for you." There's a lot of "That depends on what you're looking for" in the answer, so let's break it down. I'm presuming, by the way, that those reading this are primarily interested in buying their first dutch oven. If you've already got one or two and you're looking to buy another, you'll still be looking for the same basic things, but your reasons for buying will be different, and you could possibly have a different result.

You'll want to consider four basic variables when you're deciding which kind to buy: the type, size, material, and quality.

Type

You have two basic options: camp dutch ovens, or stove dutch ovens. Which you choose will depend on what you're going to do with it.

A camp dutch oven is primarily designed for outdoor cooking using wood coals or charcoal briquettes. It has a lip around the perimeter of the lid that keeps the coals on the lid and prevents ash from falling down into the food when you lift it. It also has legs on the bottom that lift the dutch oven up above any coals you want to put underneath it.

A stove dutch oven is designed primarily for use indoors in a conventional oven or on your stovetop. It won't have the legs, because you're setting it in your oven or resting directly on your stove's burner. It doesn't have the lip around the lid, because no coals will be put on top. Some of these will even be coated in colored enamels.

It *is* possible to use a camp dutch oven indoors, but it's not as convenient. It's also possible to use a stove dutch oven outdoors, but it's tricky.

Size

Dutch ovens are primarily measured by diameter, and sometimes by quart capacity. Common sizes are 10 and 12 inches. You can buy them as small as 5 inches or as large as 22 inches (which take considerable effort to lift, even without food in them). Which one you end up buying will depend largely on who you'll be cooking for. If you're cooking for yourself or have a small family, you won't want one that's big. If you have a large family or are thinking you'll end up cooking for groups, you'll want one bigger.

If this is your first oven and you're just interested in experimenting a little, I'd recommend a 12-inch shallow oven. This will have the capacity to feed a family of four with some leftovers and can easily cook for a gathering of as many as eight, depending on what you're cooking. Breads, stews, chilies, desserts, and even small roasts can easily be done in a 12-inch dutch oven.

Larger and smaller ovens will come in handy in more specialized situations. For example, I use my 14-inch ovens to cook turkeys and larger specialty meats. My 8-inch dutch oven I use for sides of rice or sauces.

Material

There are two basic materials used to make dutch ovens: cast iron and aluminum. Both have their advantages and disadvantages. Even though all of my dutch ovens are cast iron, I've seen chefs that swear by each one.

Cast iron is probably the most popular. It's the historic choice. It heats evenly (if slowly) and holds the heat very well, so your food stays warm in it, even after it's done cooking. It can also take a lot of heat without damage. Unfortunately, it's very heavy, and the bigger the oven, the heavier it is. Cast iron has to be seasoned to be used effectively, but with regular use, that seasoning patina gets better and better, and it becomes non-stick. Cast iron also lasts forever.

Aluminum dutch ovens are much lighter than cast iron, so they are often the pot of choice for campers, river runners, and backpackers that carry their gear in to their campsites. It won't rust, so you don't need to season it. It heats up quickly, but that also means that it cools quickly and is prone to developing hot spots.

Some say that cast iron-cooked food tastes better, but I've tasted delicious food from both kinds.

Quality

The best dutch ovens I've ever seen come from two companies: Lodge and Camp Chef. There are lots of smaller brands, like Texsport, and even a few that are no-name. You can often come across dutch ovens at yard sales and antique stores. Some dutch oven chefs I know will swear by one brand or another. While it's true that some are better made, keep in mind that our pioneer ancestors cooked successfully in dutch ovens made hundreds of years before modern companies were formed and contemporary casting procedures were invented. I've cooked delicious meals in off-brand dutch ovens. I prefer my lodge, but you can be successful with anything.

Hints for Checking Quality

First, check to see that the lid fits well. Press down on the lip of the lid all the way around. If you find a spot where the lid rocks back and forth, that's a sign of a poorly fitting lid. That will let more moisture escape when you're cooking. Again, you can still cook well in that pot, but it won't be as effective.

Some off-brands will use different alloys or different sources for their cast iron stock. This can make for variations in the thickness of the pot, as well as in the density of the metal. In either case, this can cause uneven heating and hot spots. Unfortunately, you can't really check for that in the store. It's one reason why you might want to go with a more respected brand.

Still, my forefathers who crossed the plains didn't have a Lodge or a Camp Chef.

Summing It All Up

Okay, so this is really a $75 answer to a $10 question. What dutch oven should I buy? My recommendation is that if you're wanting to get started in outdoor dutch oven cooking, get a 12-inch shallow Lodge or Camp Chef. You'll possibly notice that almost all of the recipes in my blog use that basic size. My two 12ers are the workhorses of my cast iron collection.

Whatever you end up buying, now you have some knowledge to help you make a wise choice to either get started or expand once you've gotten a few recipes down!

TOOLS, SUPPLIES

Here are a few tools and supplies that you'll either need or want to acquire for great dutch oven dinners. Don't go crazy spending money right off, just get the basics first.

Lid Lifter

The whole point of this effort will be to get the dutch oven really hot to cook your food. So, you'll need some ways to handle the dutch oven without actually handling it. The best tool in your kit for this will be some kind of lid lifter.

There are commercial lid lifters made by companies all over, and they basically come down to two types: the Mair style and the hook style. The hook is the most common and the simplest. It's just a metal bar bent into a hook. Some of these also include a t-cross bar welded on. This helps stabilize the lid as you're lifting it so that you don't tip coal ash into your food. Some people refer to the hook style as the *campfire pepper* and just get on with it. I prefer to minimize it as much as possible since I like the taste of real pepper much better.

In recent years, a brand named Mair has come along with a really great design for a lid lifter. It hooks under the lid loop, like the hook-style, but it has a clamp-like motion with three legs that grip the lid tight. This makes the lid even more stable and less likely to shake ash into your food. You can lift the lid without tipping it.

Now, I've used both, and I think they both work well. You can buy them in a variety of lengths. Using the longer ones means you don't have to bend down as far to get the lid off, and using the shortest ones means that your hands are a lot closer to the heat of the coals. I think the midrange lengths are the most useful overall. Speaking for myself, I prefer the stability of the Mair-style lifters.

However . . .

I've also seen people, in the absence of anything fancy, use a pair of pliers or vice-grips, or even a hammer hook. It's kind of amazing what you can use if you're clever and resourceful. You don't have to spend a lot of money.

When the dinner is all cooked and done, any of these options can also be used with the wire bail on a dutch oven to lift and carry the oven to the hungry masses. The wire bails are also close to the coals and get very hot as well.

Charcoal Tongs

You'll be shifting red-hot glowing coals from your burning stack and putting them under and on top of your dutch oven. I know this may surprise you, but I don't recommend doing this with your bare hands. I don't know—it has to do with staying out of the local hospital's burn ward, and insurance issues . . .

Get some longer food tongs (about a foot and a half, at least), with some kind of spring-opening action. This will allow you to grab as many as two or three burning coals at a time and move them exactly where you want them. Once the coals are on the dutch oven, or the cooking surface, you can push them around with the tongs as well for exact placement. I like them a bit longer, because that keeps my hands far away from the radiant heat of a stack of burning coals, which can get more intense than you might think.

IMPORTANT NOTE: Once you use a set of tongs for moving coals, *do not* use them to move, stir, or handle food in any way. The tongs will get gunky and coated with lots of the burned and unburned chemicals that the charcoal briquettes carry. Have separate set if you're going to be touching food with them. By the way, I like the shorter handled ones for food moving.

These next items are good to have but not absolutely necessary.

Tables

You can purchase and use several different cooking surfaces. One is a low metal table, about a foot or so high. It keeps the heat up off the ground and means that I don't have to stoop down as far. They're easy to disassemble and transport. They can support a lot of weight and are good for stacking up the ovens. I like them a lot.

Adjustable height metal tables are also available that are much higher. They raise the level of the dutch oven up to waist height. They come in varying widths as well. Some will fit two ovens side-by-side, and others will fit three. Many have removable wind screens. I also like these, but they're more money.

Lid Rest/Trivet

Sometimes, when you lift the lid, you want to work with the food, and sometimes that takes two hands. Where are you going to put the lid while you're working? Don't set it on the ground! That will get the underside dirty, and that dirt falls into the food.

A lid rest is a small metal stand, raised up off the ground a bit, that you can set the lid on. It's not complicated, but it does have a couple of great additional uses. It can be put in the center of a circle of coals, and the lid can be put on it inverted. Then the lid can be heated and used as a griddle for pancakes, bacon, eggs, or tortillas. My son used this strategy to make crepes, much to my surprise.

Whisk Brush

When you're doing long cooks, like roasts and things, as you're replenishing the coals above and below your dutch oven, you'll accumulate thick piles of ash. It's good to dust that stuff away, because it can lessen the heat transfer and also block the airflow underneath. For this, you'll need a good hand whisk broom.

Here's the hard part. It must be a natural reed broom. Plastic bristles will melt right away when you use them around the hot coals and lid. The natural reed bristles will singe, but they won't melt or burn in use. They're not expensive—a few bucks—but I have a hard time finding them. I've checked all the supermarkets, megamarts, and dollar stores around my area, and they're just not to be found. There are a few places online that sell them though.

Chimney

A chimney is a pretty common item to find, and most people are probably familiar with it, especially if they've ever done any charcoal grilling. It's a metal cylinder with holes, particularly at the base, and some sort of mesh or holey metal barrier about a third of the way up on the inside. It will also have some kind of handle structure attached to the side.

The idea is that you can put newspaper in the space under the barrier, put some charcoal briquettes in the space above it, and light the newspaper. The flames from the newspaper should light the charcoal, and the rising hot air (flowing through the holes in the base) should carry the heat and flames upward to light the coals.

Using a chimney should make it possible to light your coals without using harsh chemical accelerants, like lighter fluid.

Now, I've always had trouble with the ones I've bought. I can't seem to get them to light well. The newspaper burns away, and the coals still aren't lit. So, I still end up using lighter fluid. I've heard a few suggestions to make the chimneys work better.

One suggestion is to liberally drizzle the newspaper with cooking oil. I'm told that this will make the paper burn longer. Another idea is to keep some instant-light charcoal on hand and put a few briquettes of it at the bottom of your chimney first.

I also suspect that if there are holes up the side of your chimney, it will have better ventilation.

I like to do a couple of things with a chimney, and that's why I use one anyway. It holds the heat in a nice column, so the coals get white a bit quicker. It's a great way to keep fresh coals going. I simply keep a few burning coals in the bottom of the chimney, add a dozen or so fresh coals, mix them up, and in 15 minutes or so, I have more coals to replenish my dutch ovens.

I've also developed a cool method of shaking the chimney to rotate the coals, allowing more even burning. It takes a flick of the wrist when I shake the chimney upward, tossing the coals forward to back, and turning over the entire column of coals.

Gloves

Heavy gloves are very useful when handling extremely hot things. They are convenient when you are lifting a dutch oven or trying to empty it out. Simple hot pads can work too, but having the protection actually *on* your hands means that you don't have to worry about anything slipping. Several dutch oven companies make heavy leather gloves, and you can find them in hardware stores all over as well.

Tripod

This is a great tool if you want to cook soup or chili over an open, active fire. The tall metal tripod has a chain hanging down to hook to the bail wire of the dutch oven. You can easily adjust the heat by adjusting the length of the chain.

There are many more options: dutch oven liners, tote bags, and even Christmas tree ornaments. Believe me, if you have money to spend, somewhere there is someone willing to take it from you. In most cases, you'll get something good for your money, but always ask yourself if you really *need* the item you're spending all that cash on. I remind myself that my ancestors didn't have any of these things, and they still cooked well.

HEAT

It was an interesting revelation to me to suddenly realize that cooking is simple. I mean, we've been doing it for thousands and thousands of years. There are lots of ways to do it. Lots of different kinds of ovens, stoves, hearths, grills, and griddles. But the bottom line is that you're applying heat to food. How you do that and how much of it you do has varied over the centuries. But still, that's all you're doing.

In the dutch oven world, you do it by burning something. That can be wood burned down to coals, or it can be commercially made charcoal briquettes. For my backyard kitchen, I use briquettes, because they're easy to control and easy to light. If you use the good brands, they'll burn long and steady. The cheap ones give off inconsistent heat and burn out too fast. You don't need fancy mesquite or smoke flavoring, because none of that will get through the iron to the food anyway.

In most dutch oven recipes, you need heat coming up from the bottom, and heat coming down from the top. The camp dutch ovens have a lip around the lid that keeps the coals on top and the ash out of your food.

Here's a chart to show you how many coals to use on the different dutch oven sizes to get a desired approximate temperature.

Size	300⁰	325⁰	350⁰	375⁰	400⁰	425⁰	450⁰	475⁰
8″	12–14	13–16	15–18	17–19	18–20	19–21	20–23	21–24
10″	16–18	18–21	20–23	23–25	24–26	25–28	27–30	28–32
12″	19–22	22–25	25–28	27–29	28–32	30–33	33–36	36–40
14″	24–28	27–31	30–33	32–35	35–38	38–41	40–43	43–47

To use the table, simply cross-reference the size of the dutch oven with the heat required. That will give you the number of total coals to use. Then you can split it 33/66 or 50/50, for the top and bottom, depending on the cooking style you're using at the moment. This is a good reference number, but I don't hold fast to it. Also, I tend to start with a few extra coals anyway.

If you're boiling or simmering, put all the coals on the bottom *or* a third above and two thirds below.

If you're baking, put two thirds above and a third below.

If you're roasting, split the coals evenly on the top and the bottom.

If it's a windy day, a hot day, or a cold day (I like to dutch oven even in the winter) that will change. Cold weather requires more briquettes. Windy days get more air to the coals, so there's more heat, but the coals burn faster. If you have a bigger dutch oven, obviously you'll require more heat.

The recipes in this book list how many coals to put where. Truly, the best way to learn heat management is by experience. Just try it! I hold my hand over the ovens about a foot or so in the air. I've learned how hot that feels. I can tell how the weather conditions of the day are changing the temperature of the oven. That comes with practice.

It's also important to keep a side fire going. Charcoals burn down, and if you're doing a recipe that takes longer than an hour to cook, you'll need more coals to add back to your ovens. When I light the coals to begin cooking, I light too many. More than I will need. The extras become my side fire. About a half hour into the cooking, I'll add another ten or so coals to the pile. The older coals will catch the new coals, and by the time I need more coals, I'll have them ready. I've ruined too many dishes (and at least one pie) by having my coals go out halfway through. By rotating my coals through a side fire, I can cook almost indefinitely.

It's also good to be careful how you place the coals. In most cases, You want to focus the heat on the rim of the oven. Set the bottom coals in a ring around the bottom edge of the oven. You want the coals fully under the oven but not so much in the middle. Do the same on top as much as possible. This makes the heat travel down and up the sides of the oven and radiate toward the center. Coals in the middle tend to create hot spots, which will burn the food. This is usually less critical on the lid where the heat isn't directly touching the food, but it's still best to follow these recommendations.

It's good to have some long-handled tongs to grab and place the coals. Don't use your hands, obviously. It's also good to get some long-handled pliers for lifting the lid to check on the food, or an actual lid lifter.

For simmering, you've got liquid in the bottom of the oven that's going to disperse the heat, so I just pack the coals in any way I can under the oven. When I roast, I still try to keep a bit clear of the center, but more coals need to be on the bottom, so you'll have to pack them in more. A second ring works, and some people go with a sort of checkerboard pattern.

Remember, all you're doing is applying heat to food. Do it a few times and you'll get better and better at it.

SEASONING A DUTCH OVEN

For those who are new to dutch oven cooking, the *patina* is the deep, rich black coating that builds up on a dutch oven over time. It keeps the iron from rusting and the food from sticking. I'm dead serious when I say that a well-seasoned dutch oven is a better nonstick pan than most Teflon.

The patina is made from carbonized oils. The heat bakes layer after layer of carbonized oil into the pores of the iron. I've also read that it makes for better heat transfer from the pot to the food.

One day, I noticed that for some reason, the patina on a particular dutch oven was flaking off. That's a bit of a problem, but not too much. If the Teflon flakes off your skillet, you throw it away or give it to Goodwill. If the patina flakes off your cast iron, you just remake it.

So, that's what I'd decided to do.

As I mentioned before, most dutch ovens are seasoned in the factory, but there are many brands that are still sold unseasoned. You may also manage to acquire an old oven that needs reseasoning. From time to time, I'll reseason mine as well when needed.

First of all, the dutch oven needs to be prepared. If it's newly bought and unseasoned, it will probably be coated with a layer of wax to keep it from rusting. This can be scrubbed off using hot tap water.

If this is a rescued piece, it might have to be scrubbed more intensely. I mentioned previously that you shouldn't clean your dutch oven using metal scrapers, scrubbers, or harsh detergents, because that will take off the patina. At this point, however, you can use any of these, because the whole point is to take off any of the old patina and any rust that might be there as well.

Cast iron can be seasoned in many ways. You'll be heating up oil until it literally burns onto the surface of the metal, so there will be smoke. For this reason, I like to do it outdoors, in my gas grill.

I start by firing up my grill and removing the upper level grill racks to make room for the dutch ovens. I have a thermometer on the lid of my grill, so it's easy to track the temperature (assuming it's accurate). My goal is to heat them up to 400 degrees. I put the pot part of the dutch ovens upside down, without the lids, onto the grill. I set the lids on the legs of the upturned pots. I just let them heat up, with the grill lid down to trap the heat.

When they're at 350 degrees and climbing to 400, I pull the dutch ovens off the grill and set them on my back porch. I spread a layer of shortening over each one, inside and out, lids, legs, and all. It was tricky putting on the grease, because the pots were very hot. If I'm not careful, I end up touching a pot a little and get zinged. This happens especially if the melted shortening soaks through the paper towel or cloth I'm using to spread it.

Once they're coated, I put the pots back on the grill in the same way I did when I heated them up, and I close the lid again.

After about 20 minutes, I open up the grill, and the pots have a smooth, night-black patina on them. I turn off the gas and leave the grill lid open for them to cool a little. After a few minutes, while the dutch ovens are still hot, I pull them off the grill and coat them again with another thin layer of shortening.

I leave them on the back porch to fully cool. You could do a second coating, but I find that one coating gets them started. Then just use your oven a lot, and it will build up again over time.

As I was seasoning my ovens and thinking about writing this section, it occurred to me that how I put my ovens away is one of the reasons they need more seasonings. I've heard a lot of different ways to clean and store dutch ovens.

My method is to scrape out the food (not too difficult since it's so nonstick) and spray the dutch oven with very hot water. I sometimes scrub it with a plastic bristled brush. I wipe it off with paper towels. Then, while it's still somewhat hot, I spread a thin layer of oil (usually canola) over the entire surface and put the oven away.

I've heard of ovens going rancid with the oil, but that's usually because of longer-term storage, and I'm using these things at least every other week. Some of them I use weekly, or even twice a week.

I've heard of people cleaning them out and then reheating them. I even watched one friend of mine scrub his out with salt granules. I was amazed to see that it worked really well!

BABY YOU CAN LIGHT MY FIRE

—Or—

Is it Chili in here, or is it just me?

Imagine that there's an early hominid wandering through a forest. It's a nice day. He's been hunting, but he hasn't found anything for dinner just yet. He sees a small plant with a number of dangling red fruity things on it. They're not as long as his finger, and they're about that big around. He's seen things like it before, but never this exact thing. Other fruity things he's eaten have tasted really good—kinda sweet, sometimes with a bit of tang. So, he pulls a few off. They feel lighter than most fruits, almost as if they were hollow. Still, he lifts one up to his mouth and takes a bite.

Immediately his mouth floods with pain, as if it were on fire. His eyes tear and his face feels flushed and hot. All he can think of is getting something to cool the burning on his tongue. He sees a stream nearby and rushes to it, cupping the precious, cool water in his hands. Each drink cools the heat and calms the pain, but only for a moment, so he drinks more and more.

Finally, he stops, because it isn't helping. But it's not long before the pain begins to subside, and he shakes his head and walks away, a valuable lesson learned.

Today, of course, we know of the evolutionary value of a defense mechanism like this. If everyone who tries to eat you ends up screaming in pain, you don't get eaten very often. Your species lives and reproduces.

But that only works if the predators are smart. And, we're dealing with humans here, or the ancestors of them. Humans are not known for taking lessons well. See, because somewhere along the evolutionary line, one of our great-great-great-great-(etc.)-grandparents actually went *back* to that burning bush and ate those peppers a *second time*!

Maybe he just gave them to a friend so he could laugh as the victim of his prank danced and guzzled as he had done the first time. But, no matter, at some point someone decided that this burning blaze on his tongue, this fiery feeling, was a good thing.

And that's why, today, we have hot sauce.

I recently saw a video that explains why 1) peppers burn our mouths, and 2) why it feels so good afterward. It's a fascinating video and article, and in summary, it says that the capsaicin molecules in the peppers (which actually cause the heat) react with the nerve receptors on our tongues and fool them into reacting as if they'd actually touched something physically scalding hot. Our minds actually think that our tongue is scalding.

The reason water doesn't help is that the capsaicin is an oil, so the water doesn't wash it off. It only temporarily tells the tongue's nerve receptors that they're cool. Then, when the water's gone and swallowed, the heat comes back, because the capsaicin is still there.

That heat and pain also automatically trigger our body's response, which is pain relief. Endorphins! That's why you feel flushed and excited afterward. In fact, a few pain creams and ointments utilize capsaicin to topically trigger the body's natural pain relievers.

It's interesting to note that, according to the article, the menthol in mint and mint candies work the opposite way, fooling your tongue into thinking it's touching something cool.

Wow. Knowledge is cool . . .

Or is it hot?

I was curious to find out how spiciness and heat are measured.

There are a number of ways, but the most common of all is the Scoville scale. It's named after pharmacist Wilbur Scoville, who developed this method of testing and measuring in 1912.

Here's how it works. When you want to test a pepper variety, or even a crop, some of the peppers are dried, and an extract is made with alcohol. That extract is then diluted with a formulated sugar and water solution until a panel of tasters no longer taste any heat. The measure, then, is how much dilution there has to be to tame the peppery beast.

The system works, but there are a lot of variables. First of all, since the tasters are humans, there will be variances from testing group to testing group. It's not empirical, like counting the actual capsaicin molecules would be. Second, even the same variety of pepper will not measure the same. Soil, climate, and many other factors will impact the heat of a given pepper crop. So, not all jalapenos are created equal.

In addition, those eating the pepper or the dish will have different tolerances to heat. Some of that's born in, and some of it changes with age, and in some cases, the eater's own experiences with hot can make perceptions vary. For example, someone who eats hot food on a daily basis won't be phased by a milder pepper that would make a lightweight run screaming for the water fountain.

As if that isn't variation enough, the preparation of the pepper can impact its heat, too, like pickling and other such things.

Still, it's good to have a relative scale. The following will guide you in making choices about what kind of heat to use, and how much of it to use.

SCOVILLE HEAT UNITS—EXAMPLES
No significant heat—**bell pepper**, aji dulce
100–900—pimento, **peperoncini**, banana pepper, cubanelle
1,000–2,500—anaheim pepper, poblano pepper, rocotillo pepper, peppadew, sriracha sauce, gochujang
3,500–8,000—espelette pepper, **jalapeño pepper**, **chipotle**, **smoked jalapeño**, guajillo pepper, new mexican peppers, hungarian wax pepper, tabasco sauce, fresno pepper
10,000–23,000—**serrano pepper**, peter pepper, aleppo pepper
30,000–50,000—guntur chilli, **cayenne pepper**, ají pepper, tabasco pepper, cumari pepper (capsicum chinese)
50,000–100,000—byadgi chilli, bird's eye chili, malagueta pepper, chiltepin pepper, piri piri (african bird's eye), pequin pepper, siling labuyo
100,000–350,000—habanero chili, scotch bonnet pepper, datil pepper, rocoto, piri piri ndungu, madame jeanette, peruvian white habanero, jamaican hot pepper, guyana wiri Wiri, fatalii
350,000–580,000—red savina habanero
855,000–1,463,700—naga viper pepper, infinity chilli, bhut jolokia chili pepper (ghost pepper), trinidad scorpion butch t pepper, bedfordshire super naga, 7-pot chili
1,500,000–2,000,000 trinidad moruga scorpion, carolina reaper

With this chart as a general guide, you can experiment with various chilies and various amounts of heat. The ones in bold are the ones that I, personally, like and use the most.

I've been using hot peppers and other such things since I started cooking, and, while I don't know everything, I have picked up a few practical tips. So, here are my tips for cooking with heat.

1. Decide in advance what you're shooting for. Are you cooking what will be a four-alarm chili, or do you just want to liven up a previously tame beef stew? Just a little heat will pick up a dish, often without it being perceptibly hot. On the other hand, sometimes you want to scorch out your mouth. In either case, decide beforehand rather than arrive there by accident or default.

2. Start with less and add as you go. It's easy to add more heat, but it's impossible to take it out. That's why it's best to go tame at first and then build it up, tasting along the way, until you get where you want to be. Because of the variations, you won't be able to rely on a recipe, since "2 tsp. chili powder" will not always be consistent. It's also best, if possible, to let the recipe cook and simmer a bit between each tasting. That way the flavors have some time to blend in.

3. Different peppers have unique flavors, as well as different amounts of heat. Get to know them as much as you can. I really like the flavor of cayenne, for example, but I'm not as fond of jalapeno.

4. Much of the capsaicin is in the seeds and the core, so you can tame a chili significantly by cutting those away. You can do a lot of adjusting that way, too. For example, maybe one jalapeno is not enough, but two is too much. Add one in, and core the second.

5. Use gloves while handling chili, and don't wipe your eyes. I have learned this by sad experience. You know the self-defence sprays that you blast in an attacker's face? That's chili extract. If you're working with chilies and you wipe your eyes with capsaicin oil on your fingers, you're going to be in for a world of hurt. Use gloves, and throw them away when you're done.

Here's one final bit on chilies. A few years ago, I was at a roadside produce stand as fall approached. They were selling lots of different things, but I found a big basket of serrano chilies. I had this idea, so I bought a few pounds. I brought them home and laid them out on a baking tray and dried them (make sure they are completely dry, with no moisture). I broke off the stems and chewed them up in one of those little Magic Bullet blenders where you invert the cup over the blade. Presto, homemade chili powder. In subsequent years, I've found that I like to blend different chilies together in that mix. I'll usually do some serranos, some jalapenos, and some anaheims. Commercial chili powders will often include other things like garlic powder or oregano, but I prefer to add those into a dish separately.

If you do this, here are two tips.

1. I tried it in my big tabletop Ninja blender, but it didn't get the particles fine enough. Once it got them chopped to a certain point, it just tossed the chunks around. The smaller blender went faster and chopped finer into a real powder.

2. Breathe carefully or wear a surgical mask. It will burn your nose and throat if you don't.

I hope this information has helped you get a better grasp on how to use heat and peppers in your dishes. Don't be afraid of them, but use them judiciously, and they'll serve you well!

FLAVORED OILS

For a picture of this idea, scan this QR code:

One year for the holidays, I got the cool idea to make some flavored olive oils and give them to some of my cookin' friends as Christmas gifts. I did a bit of research and found some good flavor combinations. I settled on three: cinnamon and nutmeg, italian seasonings, and chili and onions.

I had a difficult time finding bottles for my adventure. I wanted the ones that have the little metal spouts. The ones I found were hard to grip once the bottle neck got oily. I eventually discovered that once you've poured in the oil, if you dry the inside of the neck thoroughly with a paper towel, the rubber in the stoppers sticks again. So, I was good to go. I got the bottles at a dollar store, so the biggest expense was the oil.

Ooops!

Those friends who got them for Christmas are probably reading this.

Anyway, I made several sets of the three oils so I could give many away and keep one for myself. I started off with cinnamon. I put about two teaspoons of nutmeg in the bottom of the bottle and dropped in a couple of cinnamon bark sticks. Then I poured in the oil. Finally, I wiped dry the inside of the neck and put on the cap. It was that simple.

For the italian-style oil, I got some sprigs of fresh herbs (basil, thyme, and oregano) and bruised them up a little. I'd read that this allows for more infusion of flavor. I put them into the bottle. I sliced up a couple of cloves of fresh garlic for each bottle and put in some dried tomatoes. I filled them with oil, cleaned them, and capped them.

The chili-flavored oil was also easy to make. I bought some thin, red chilies (dried) in the Mexican section of the supermarket. I also sliced up some pearl onions and added those. Then in went the oil.

Once you've made the oils, set them aside and let the flavors infuse for three to four weeks. Best idea? Make them the day after thanksgiving!

They were a lot of fun to make, and they looked classy as well.

ADDITIONAL RECIPES & NOTES

ADDITIONAL RECIPES & NOTES

ADDITIONAL RECIPES & NOTES

INDEX

T

V

W

Z

ABOUT THE AUTHOR

MARK HANSEN started cooking in his dutch ovens in 2006 when his wife surprised him with one as a Father's Day present. His first cooking attempt was pizza, and the family instantly declared it a success! He began a tradition of cooking the family's Sunday dinners in his dutch ovens.

In April of the following year, he thought he should start sharing what he learned, and he established marksblackpot.com. Years later, and hundreds of recipes since, it's still one of the most widely read dutch oven blogs on the Internet.

Mark lives in Eagle Mountain, Utah, with his wife, Jodi, and two boys, who are also budding chefs.

OTHER DUTCH OVEN BOOKS BY MARK HANSEN

Best of the Black Pot
Black Pot for Beginners
Around the World in a Dutch Oven
Stop, Drop, and Cook
Dutch Oven Breads

0 26575 18984 1

http://www.marksblackpot.com/